Total Memory Makeover

Also by Marilu Henner

Wear Your Life Well

Healthy Holidays/Party Hearty

Healthy Kids

Healthy Life Kitchen

I Refuse to Raise a Brat

The 30-Day Total Health Makeover

Marilu Henner's Total Health Makeover

By All Means Keep On Moving

Total Memory Makeover

UNCOVER YOUR PAST,
TAKE CHARGE OF YOUR FUTURE

MARILU HENNER

with Lorin Henner

GALLERY BOOKS

New York   London   Toronto   Sydney   New Delhi

Gallery Books

G A Division of Simon & Schuster, Inc.
1230 Avenue of the Americas
New York, NY 10020

Copyright © 2012 by Marilu Henner

All rights reserved, including the right to reproduce this book or portions thereof in any form whatsoever. For information address Gallery Books Subsidiary Rights Department, 1230 Avenue of the Americas, New York, NY 10020

First Gallery Books hardcover edition February 2012

GALLERY BOOKS and colophon are registered trademarks of Simon & Schuster, Inc.

For information about special discounts for bulk purchases, please contact Simon & Schuster Special Sales at 1-866-506-1949 or business@simonandschuster.com

The Simon & Schuster Speakers Bureau can bring authors to your live event. For more information or to book an event contact the Simon & Schuster Speakers Bureau at 1-866-248-3049 or visit our website at www.simonspeakers.com.

Designed by Joy O'Meara

Manufactured in the United States of America

10   9   8   7   6   5   4   3

Library of Congress Cataloging-in-Publication Data

Henner, Marilu.
    Total memory makeover : uncover your past, take charge of your future / Marilu Henner ; with Lorin Henner. —1st hbk. ed.
        p.   cm.
    1. Memory.   I. Henner, Lorin.   II. Title.
BF378.A87H46   2012
153.1'2—dc23   2011052489

ISBN 978-1-4516-5121-8
ISBN 978-1-4516-5124-9 (ebook)

To my memorable guys, Michael, Nick, and Joey

Contents

Contents

Acknowledgments

I would like to thank the following people for their love and encouragement (and help!) throughout this daunting, but, ultimately, gratifying process.

I had always wanted to write a memory book, but it wasn't until the *60 Minutes* story that people really understood what HSAM was. None of that would have been possible had it not been for the ever-impressive Lesley Stahl. Just writing her name, many of the images from our almost twenty-eight years of friendship come flooding in, so I'll stop here and just say a huge thank you, Lesley. You are not only a force of nature, you are also the godmother of all things HSAM. Her remarkable team at *60 Minutes:* the fearless Shari Finkelstein who started this process as the skeptical producer, but continues on as a true friend; the ebullient Jennie Held whose phone calls were always a blast; to Matthew Lev who was helpful to their team during this process and David Rubin who was the first person who told me, "You're going to be known for this more than for *Taxi!*"

To the great man himself, Dr. James McGaugh, whose scientific brilliance put a name to HSAM which has now opened up a whole new world of research for so many people. To Nan Collett, the true heartbeat of HSAM, and to Larry Cahill, Craig E. L. Stark, Frithjof R. Kruggel, Heather Anson, Aaron Mattfeld, and of course, the tireless and tenacious Aurora K. R. LePorte.

My fellow HSAMers: Louise Owen, Bob Petrella, Jill Price, Brad Williams, and the late Rick Baron, who share with me this unusual gift. No matter how many other people they find (and I hope they find many), we'll always have Irvine!

To my incredible literary agent at WME, Mel Berger, our eighth book together and definitely the one we bonded over the most. Thank you (and your fabulous assistant, Hadley Franklin) for always being there. And to Theresa Brown for being not only my agent but a THM friend.

To my style idol and new BFF, the inimitable Jen Bergstrom, publisher extraordinaire at Simon & Schuster and her outstanding team including the powerhouse Kate Dresser, Heather Hunt, Emily Drum, Jeremie Ruby-Strauss, Emilia Pisani, Louise Burke, Sally Franklin, John Paul Jones, Lisa Litwack, Paul Olsewsky, Joy O'Meara, Larry Pekarek, Aja Pollack, and Jennifer Weidman. And, of course, the dynamic duo of publicity super heroes, Jennifer Robinson (Simon & Schuster) and Susan Madore (Guttman Associates).

To my literally *Unforgettable* gang, Ed Redlich, John Bellucci, Sarah Timberman, Carl Beverly, Mike Foley, Jan Nash, John David Coles, Merrill Karpf, Erik Oleson, Jean DeSegonzac, Brian Beneker, Christal Henry, Dylan Walsh, Michael Gaston, Kevin Rankin, Daya Vaidya, Alexis Genya, Spencer Hudnut, Heather Bellson, Paul Holahan, Jim Adler, Steven Maeda, Alicia Kirk, Jane Curtin and the ever-impressive Poppy Montgomery who makes HSAM look better than ever.

To my incredible agents at Innovative Artists, the unstoppable Jonathan Howard, the devilish Nevin Dolcefino, the elegant Marcia Hurwitz, and the charming Mary Douris, and to Deb (the determinator) Goldfarb of Rebel Entertainment.

To my extraordinary team (and buddies) at Marilu.com, the unbeatable Tonia Kulberda, Teresa Canter, Jill Nelson, Kecia Newton, Angela Pelletier, Stephanie Simmons, Alyse Stanley, and DeeAnn Wehner who all contributed their time and testimonials to this book, especially the ever-adorable MaryBeth Borkowski who read several drafts and critiqued it with her usual English teacher expertise and largesse of spirit.

To my closest "friends for life" whose stories and quotes were heartfelt *and* funny (no easy task!): the incomparable Caroline Aaron, the dynamic Tony Danza, the outrageous Sharon Feldstein, the one-of-a-kind Jim Jacobs, and the soulful Jim Canning whose words inspired the tone of this book. And to Aimee Liu, who thanks to Tony's recommendation, gave a fresh perspective right when it was needed most.

To my beautiful sister Jo Ann Carney, who was never too busy to brainstorm about the book and to share her memories and ideas, her totally original husband William Drake, who gave me one of the best quotes ever, to my scrappy niece Suzanne Carney, a talented writer in her own right who read an early draft and was so loving and encouraging; to my unflappable sister Christal Henner, whose daily calls are my touchstone and reality check, not only while writing this book, but throughout my entire life. And to my ex-husband, Rob Lieberman, who has shared with me twenty-seven years of memories (sixteen together) that continue on with our boys and our friendship.

To my multitalented assistant Jessica Davis, who jumped into the process with a can-do spirit and an open heart. Is there anything you can't do?

To my darling sister-in-law Kaisha Henner for her research and writing skills, who kept everything in line including Lorin, while managing to pull off being a beautiful bride at the best wedding ever! How did you do that? To my hilariously talented favorite co-author and memory subject, Lorin Henner, this is our ninth book together and by far, the most challenging. Thank you for everything you do to make this work despite long distances, construction noises, different schedules, cat hospital visits and your wedding. You would be my friend, even if you weren't my brother (And thank God for Skype!).

And most of all, to my three guys, who would make life memorable, even without HSAM. My effervescent, but laser-focused son Joey, who is the funniest person in our family; my son Nick, whose academic prowess is surpassed only by his insight and his honesty. (I could not have done this book without you.) To my loving husband Michael, there are no words to describe how I feel about you and our life together. I am eternally grateful for every day I get to spend with you making new memories (and I'm so glad you're finally a believer!).

With great love and appreciation to all!

Foreword

As Marilu Henner tells us in this book, memories can indeed be unforgettable, perhaps not in every way, but in highly interesting and important ways. Most of us can try to remember the many details of experiences long past, and we do, in fact, remember some of them, sometimes. But mostly we forget.

Marilu is different: Most of her long-past experiences are highly preserved and readily recalled. She is one of a dozen or so individuals who have been identified as having "Highly Superior Autobiographical Memory" (HSAM). Those of us who study her memory, and the memories of the few others we have identified as having HSAM, strongly believe that understanding the brain processes that enable such extraordinary memory may provide new insights into how our brains create and maintain memories, including ordinary ones. Memory is, of course, our most important personal capacity. Insights into the nature of HSAM could ultimately have critical implications for understanding why most of us mostly forget and, additionally, may eventually provide suggestions for dealing with disorders that compromise memory.

This book is like no other book about memory, and the insights offered are unique. In these pages, we learn from Marilu what it is like to have such a memory, why it is important to her, and why she thinks we can all benefit by taking steps to improve our own remembering. Readers will learn that Marilu is as well organized as she is thoughtful, insightful, enthusiastic, and, well, delightfully humorous. The advice she offers may not turn all of us (or any of us) into HSAMers, but every reader will learn much about the importance of memory, as well as things we might do to help us maintain memories of our own personal experiences.

Enjoy reading Marilu's memory journey.

Dr. James L. McGaugh
Research Professor, Department of Neurobiology and Behavior
Fellow, Center for the Neurobiology of Learning and Memory
University of California–Irvine

Insanity is doing the same thing over and over again and expecting different results.

—*Albert Einstein*

That's not insanity; it's bad memory!

—*Marilu Henner*

Preface

One time, I was riding on a train from New York City to Philadelphia with Marilu. This was a long time ago. We were just kids, teenagers nearly, riding together on the Amtrak to Philly, making up our lives as we clicked along. So the conversation dwindled, as conversations often do between young people, and there were periods of awkward silence as the landscape flew by. Marilu was gazing out the window and suddenly remarked, "Hey, is that a junkyard?" I looked out as we flashed past what was definitely a junkyard. I mean, it was this huge field, surrounded by a metal fence and filled with junk. It could have been nothing *other* than a junkyard; that was evident. I looked back at her nervously: "Yeah, I *think* it's a junkyard . . ." Then we both looked at each other for a few seconds and started laughing, really laughing. It was the kind of laughter that indicated that you were in a friendship, a solid friendship that would last longer than the train ride. An icebreaker laugh . . . a memorable laugh.

And the friendship did last, for decades and decades. Years later, through all the tumult of growing up and growing older, I vaguely remembered that moment on the train to Philly, and I mentioned it once to Marilu, to see if she remembered it. Of course, by this time, I was aware of how precise her memory could be; it was sort of a running joke among all the people who knew her that she would remember everything. Yet this moment had occurred decades before, a silly, awkward glitch in a forgotten conversation on a train ride whose purpose was lost to time, or so I thought. But no, Marilu not only remembered the question, the laugh, the awkward realization that we were just bumbling kids on a train, she remembered everything about that day, that train ride, where we were going, who we would meet in Philly. She remembered the weather, the number of the train, the car and seat we were sitting in. She even remembered the specific junk in the junkyard. She remembered the quizzical look on my face when I said, "Yeah, I *think* it's a junkyard . . ." She remembered how long we laughed and what we said later. She remembered everything, as though the moment had been filmed and she was running the scene in her mind. It was like those videos you take of your children. You watch the film years later and all the feelings and events come back in a rush, except, for Marilu, there's no need for the video. It's all there, even the delicate emotional overlay, the awkward pause, and the release of laughter. And she can remember the day before that and the day after, and all the days that followed.

James Canning
(Marilu's friend and fellow cast member in the original and Broadway productions of *Grease*)

Introduction

*M*emory is everything! In every single moment of your life—past, present, and future—memory is involved. All that you do, all that you see, everything you learn, each person you meet, and all of your experiences have conscious meaning only insofar as you remember them. No matter how much you discover and experience today, its value vanishes if it's forgotten tomorrow. When we're young, we take memory for granted. As we get older, we genuinely fear losing it—not only because the ability itself can fade with age, but also because we are finally wise enough to know its true value. There is no human endeavor more worthy of our best efforts than the pursuit of a great memory!

Like it or not, your past is in you even if you *don't* remember it. Every single thing you have ever experienced is in you, stored somewhere on your mental hard drive. It has all been recorded in your body and on your psyche, and it is making you behave in ways that you aren't even aware of. This can often scare people, but I think it makes an excellent case for developing one's memory. You may not be consciously connecting this past information to what you are doing in the present, but you should be. You are constantly responding to *now* because of *back then*. When you are cognizant of your memories and can call upon them as needed, it keeps you from making the same mistakes over and over again and helps you avoid that pitfall Einstein called insanity. It also makes you better at sizing up situations and making the right choices, as well as understanding why you are the way you are.

There are different kinds of memory, but I am known for my autobiographical memory. Choose any random date during my lifetime (*every* day since I was twelve in 1964), and I can tell you what day of the week it was and exactly what I was doing on that day. This ability is called Highly Superior Autobiographical Memory (HSAM for short), and I am one of only twelve documented cases in the world, so far. I can't tell you what combination of nature and nurture gives someone a superior autobiographical memory, but I *can* tell you that I have learned and retained my most important life lessons from having one. But this book is not just about my memory or the feats I can accomplish with it. It is much more about what this ability has taught me and how you can use these lessons to transform *your* memory, *your* past, and ultimately, *your* future. It doesn't matter whether or not you were born with my ability. *Everyone* can remember a great deal more than they do now, and everyone can benefit in the same way that I do. All that is needed are the right tools, along with the motivation and effort required to use them.

How much would your life change if, from this moment on, you had the ability to always make the right decision in everything you did? It goes without saying that your life, anyone's life, would improve *instantly* and *dramatically*. For example, think of Bill Murray's character Phil Connors in the film *Groundhog Day*. The movie's premise is that Phil must relive the same day over and over again. Eventually, after many repetitions, Phil reexamines his selfish life and finally finds the wisest choices, best responses, and most helpful actions for every single moment within that one isolated day. And in less than twenty-four hours (twenty-four hours for everyone else, that is) he becomes the most respected and beloved man in town, gets the girl of his dreams, learns what matters most in life, and sets a course to live happily ever after.

Obviously, this is just fun Hollywood fantasy. *Nobody* in the real world bats a thousand. But, of course, that is what we aim to do. *Groundhog Day* was such a success because we would all love to make perfect choices 100 percent of the time. We all would love to have the information necessary to make the right decision in every moment of every day. I think audiences were delighted to see a character who was given the opportunity to learn from his mistakes, despite the fact that it took him repeated chances to finally get it right.

We tend to think of "the right decision" as what will ultimately get us what we want, whether it's working late for the boss, helping a friend move, hosting a dinner party, investing in a 401(k), or even destructive choices like binge drinking or cheating on a loved one. Sometimes the payoff is immediate, and other times the rewards are delayed. *Every choice* is based on some kind of incentive. Even obviously wrong choices are made with compelling motivations. Ordering a mud pie for dessert is a choice we make, because the momentary happiness we expect to receive outweighs in our minds the consequences of those butt-plumping calories. Even if we've made this mistake before, we still might not stop ourselves. It could make us sick, depressed, or unmotivated, but what is most important is that immediate gratification. Forgetting what may result from a choice is never good. For example, because of the debilitating mud pie, we might end up so tired that we skip the two-mile walk we promised ourselves in the morning. If we could actually see into the future, our choices would be easy. If we knew for a fact that this mud pie would turn out to be the world's greatest dessert experience and would inspire us to upgrade our two-mile walk to a five-mile run, the choice to indulge would be perfectly advisable. If we knew that changing careers would eventually lead to a much happier, rewarding life, then that choice would be obvious. But we never really know what will happen. That new career could become overly stressful, disappointing, or obsolete. As you can see, our happiness depends upon predicting, as accurately as possible, what will happen in the future. In order to minimize this risk, we gather information, much like Phil Connors does in *Groundhog Day*. But we don't have the luxury of do-overs. For us, the past serves as the primary source of this information. The better you remember your own experiences, the faster you will "get it," as Phil did eventually.

You could say that everything we do in life is like navigating a maze to get to the reward. Success depends on how well we know the course: where all the dead ends are, as well as all the paths that lead to success. It is easy to repeat negative behavior when we don't clearly remember the consequences of that behavior. People often say, "I'll never drink that much again," only to find themselves doing exactly that. They allow the memory of their hangover to fade. When they are given the choice to take that extra drink, they do it, because they can no longer vividly remember how they felt or the promises they made to themselves. And it's not just because alcohol dulls memory; people have the same mental block when it comes to food, work, consumer credit, exercise, and bad relationships. It takes some people a lifetime to finally accept the connection between self-indulgence and consequence, and some people *never* realize it. They never really grow up. Remembering your past in a meaningful way is synonymous with growing up.

In having HSAM, I have an immense, easily accessible, internal library of my past that I can pull from at any point. I carry my personal history in my pocket 24/7. This really does give me an advantage for predicting what will happen in my future. My decision-making process has more information to draw from and, therefore, I am better able to make sound decisions than if I didn't have that information at my fingertips. But what does that mean for *you*? Keep in mind that it's not the *ability* to remember that matters as much as the *information* itself. You don't need a superior memory, as long as you have a strategy for gathering, analyzing, and storing your life information.

As an example, every professional sports team and every successful business keeps detailed records of their past. They don't just show up every day to play the game or go to work and hope for the best. They carefully plan and strategize to put the odds in their favor, so they can achieve their objectives. In baseball, a record is kept for each player: how he performs against left-handers and right-handers, in day vs. night play, the percentage of his ball placement in the field, and so many other factors. This is how managers determine how to use their rosters, which players to start, when to switch, and which plays to call. (Think *Moneyball!*) The same strategy is used for football, basketball, boxing, tennis, and every other sport. A team couldn't even compete today without these kinds of detailed reports. Businesses work in the same way. This is what separates a successful business from an unsuccessful one. The more detailed the records are, the better future results can be predicted and controlled. Why not use these same strategies for your own life?

Now, some of you might be saying, "I don't know if I want to remember *too* much of my life!" Some people are fearful of remembering certain moments from their past. But I think we need to face the fact that this impulse to forget isn't totally healthy. Everyone has experiences from their past that they try to avoid: a death in the family, a car accident, being bullied in school or humiliated at work, a lost love, or a bad relationship. Although these are painful moments to relive in your mind, it is therapeutic and beneficial to face and understand them. Negative experiences provide the most memorable and useful lessons. (For example, one reason I'm so committed to my healthy lifestyle is that I lost my parents very young, and this fact is never far from my mind as I make healthy choices on a daily basis.) Conversely, when we avoid negative thoughts and feelings, we give them maximum significance and power. They become emotional "bogeymen." In denial, we create more pain than we do in simply confronting our memories. Allowing yourself the freedom to relive those moments helps you better understand what made them traumatic in the first place. By understanding that pain, we become better equipped to respond to similar moments in the future and resolve them in our subconscious, which helps weaken their impact. This is the way to conquer the memories you fear most. A horror film is never as scary the second time, and it's often laughable the third or fourth time you watch it. You can watch the movie with interest, rather than closing your eyes and turning away.

But there is much more to the process outlined in this book than learning from past mistakes. Equally important is remembering moments of success—for example, when we made a boss, a teacher, or a client proud and more confident in our abilities. Remembering the consequences of those choices makes us much more likely to repeat them and is key to establishing a pattern of positive behavior. Another critical benefit of remembering your life is the preservation of important moments that would have otherwise been lost or diluted. Without making a conscious effort to remember the people we care about most, those thoughts and feelings will surely fade. As the years pass, it becomes more and more difficult to evoke the endearing way your father told his favorite joke or how patiently your mother listened to your long-winded stories without ever looking bored. It's important to your self-knowledge to remember how those moments affected you and what they ultimately mean to you.

But you will never be able to remember if you are resistant to remembering. In order to be successful at remembering your past you have to develop a healthy mind-set about *wanting* to remember, and, more importantly, you have to get yourself *ready* to remember. You have to prime yourself. You cannot be unwilling to look back and relive certain feelings of abandonment or a bad breakup, or an unsettling argument with a parent, or the humiliation you felt because of a critical teacher or boss, or a terrifying experience with a bully. Something intrigued you about your past enough to compel you to pick up this book, so please don't just *read* it. Be an active and willing player and look at your past from a different perspective through wide-open eyes. For years I have heard people say things like, "I really want to lose weight and get healthy," but they would make no progress, or get even heavier and unhealthier. I now know from my own and others' experiences that no progress can be made unless one actively commits to making dramatic diet and exercise changes. This is also true for memory. The desire to remember could be there, but unless you specifically set a course to revolutionize your memory patterns, unless you commit to your Total Memory Makeover, nothing will change. Go beyond just wanting to remember or being receptive to remembering. Take action to remember.

The researchers I've been working with at UC Irvine are still determining exactly how and why HSAM exists, but everyone, whether or not they have HSAM, can document their past and learn from it. It doesn't *really* matter if the information is in your head, in your diary, or on your computer's hard drive. If it is accessible, it is useful. Think of your Total Memory Makeover as the world's most fascinating history and psychology courses rolled into one, because that's exactly what it is! Instead of studying American History or Psych 101, you are learning the history and psychology of *you*, everyone's favorite subject (let's be honest!). You are both the student *and* the subject of this course. The star of your own movie, as it were. But you've got lots of costars, too, who are also fascinating: family, coworkers, acquaintances, friends, and foes. Don't be surprised if you learn much more in this course than you ever expected.

In this course, we will start with what I like to call the Track. Your Track will be your own personal key for unlocking your past. I believe that everyone has a Track for remembering things. Your Track is usually what you care about most. For example, some people can't remember what they ate for dinner last night but can tell you precise scores, specific dates, exact stats, and detailed plays from a game they watched thirty years ago. Some people might forget sporting events they've seen (perhaps deliberately), but they can't forget a relationship, a haircut, a meal, or even how much they weighed at specific times. (Guilty!) Many people have a career or travel Track. It really depends on what is most important to them personally. *Everyone* remembers *something* exceptionally well and in great detail. Everyone has a Track.

Starting with your Track, we are going to go back and document the highlights of your life starting from childhood. Eventually you will have a fairly extensive, well-organized timeline of your life. It sounds complicated, but it's not. I will be guiding you through it every step of the way! After creating and organizing this timeline, you will then immerse yourself in the history of your life (You 101). I promise you will learn a lot more studying your own life than studying an ancient hero like Alexander the Great. The Internet alone gives you limitless possibilities to tap into your past. You can look up newspaper archives, old photographs from your neighborhood, old postcards, toys and items you formerly owned on eBay, school and church websites, and, of course, all the different social websites, like Facebook, Classmates, and Genealogy, where you can actually contact people you haven't spoken to in thirty or forty years. That is something no other generation in history has had the ability to do. Suppose you grew up in the sixties in Brooklyn and now you live in Los Angeles. With Google Earth, you can walk around your old neighborhood, step by step, house by house, and trigger thousands of childhood memories while sitting at your computer desk in Los Angeles. Even though Ed's Candy Store is now a Starbucks, it doesn't matter. In many instances, the structure is still the same. The memory triggers are still there in your neighborhood even if certain aspects have changed.

This will be good therapy, too. You can't study your life without taking a good hard look at yourself and learning from it. The past demystifies why something is working or, more likely, isn't. Positive and negative patterns in your life are easy to identify once you step back and look at them from a wide-angle perspective. Analyzing your history will help you uncover those negative and positive patterns, so that you can take charge and use them to your advantage. Undoubtedly, this will give you a whole new outlook, providing an opportunity to keep what you love, change what you dislike, and get a fresh start! You can begin making sound decisions intellectually, emotionally, creatively, financially, and spiritually. In other words, you can change *now* by remembering *then*.

Most memory books focus on mnemonic devices like acronyms, place pegs, and memory palaces to help you remember lists, definitions, names, cards, numbers, and so on. They are specifically designed to help you remember a lot of information—quickly and temporarily—for school exams, meetings at work, shopping lists, and so on. And that's great. We will be exploring various memory techniques as well, but that is not the main focus of this book. We will be going deeper than that. This book is more about self-exploration. Hopefully, you will be learning things about yourself that you didn't remember existed. You will be uncovering your past in ways that will help you make connections and remember them the next time you're faced with certain decisions. Most standard memory books, at least the honest ones, admit that memory itself is not improved. The *skill* of remembering things may improve, but there's a difference. You can get very fast at remembering a deck of cards or long lists of numbers or vocabulary words, but you will still forget where you parked your car or the details of your last birthday (or why you shouldn't marry that tempestuous on-again, off-again ex!). In addition, memory drills don't significantly improve your understanding of what you are remembering. They do help to a certain degree, but if you really want to learn with deep understanding, you still have to read, study, analyze, and experience a particular subject. There is no shortcut when it comes to learning. Memorizing definitions or the times tables or the periodic table does help as an aid and reference as you are learning those subjects, but they are not a magic pill that will help you finish medical school in three months—which would never be the goal of autobiographical memory, anyway. In short, mnemonic strategies are helpful but limited.

But please don't get me wrong. I'm not knocking mnemonics. Being able to memorize the order of a deck of cards in a minute or less is impressive, but it is not going to help you figure out why you always feel like a victim or seem to repeatedly crave drama in your life. There is a bit of a fast-food feeling to the whole process of mnemonics. They fill you up quickly but can't sustain you properly in the long run. What *is* different about this memory book is that I am not trying to help you break any speed records. This is a journey, a wonderful, joyful ride through your life, and I hope you enjoy every moment.

Are you ready for your Total Memory Makeover?

Let's get started!

Part One

ANTICIPATION

Get Ready to Remember

Chapter One

Crazy Memory

Never make your home in a place. Make a home for yourself inside your own head. You'll find what you need to fur-
nish it—memory, friends you can trust, love of learning, and
other such things. That way it will go with you wherever you
journey.

—*Tad Williams*

I grew up as one of six kids in a busy, noisy Catholic family in
a lower-middle-class neighborhood on the northwest side of Chicago. My father was in the automobile business, and my family ran
a dancing school in our garage. My mother also ran a beauty shop in
our kitchen. Everyone hung out at our house, and we were famous
for our parties. We thought of ourselves as the Kennedys of Logan
Square, and it seemed to me as if everything that happened in our
family was important and memorable. But it wasn't just because of
my family's popularity; I can see now that my father had a lot to do
with the development of my desire to remember.

One of my father's favorite sayings was "There are three parts
to every event: anticipation, participation, and recollection, and
the greatest of these is recollection!" Perhaps it was because of his

own great memory that my dad—a troubleshooter in the automobile business who made it a point to remember things about his customers—instilled in all of his kids this love for recollection. My family would spend weeks in the anticipation phase planning for one of our famous parties, imagining who was going to be there, figuring out what music would be played, what each of us would wear, the food my mom would serve, and what we all had to do to get ready for the party. The party itself (participation) was always the highlight of the season, whether it was a pool party at the Howard Johnson's Motor Lodge, a beach party at Sand-Lo Beach, a record party where everyone brought a 45 and replenished my mother's collection, or one of our famous Christmas parties with a hundred and twenty-five people packed in our garage/studio. These gatherings were always exciting, but even more fun was had the next day recounting, reliving, and analyzing everything that had transpired throughout the night before.

"Can you believe what she was wearing?" "Did you notice how much they were flirting?" "How great a dancer was that new guy?" We couldn't wait to compare notes after every big occasion. In fact, reminiscing about the party was, in itself, an event not to be missed. Friends would come over to help us clean up just to be involved in the actual party's "recollection party," which then often needed its *own* recollection party!

Recollection became my favorite part of any event, and it would certainly last longer than the participation phase, and more often than not, even longer than the anticipation. Over time, we would continue to refer back to those party images and stories and carry them through to the next event and *its* recollection.

I loved these memory sessions and began to see everything in my life in this way: anticipation, participation, and recollection (APR). At these recollection sessions and in everyday life, I was so good at remembering the smallest details about everything that happened or was taught to me that I was nicknamed Univac and the Memory Kid. As one of six children (like a litter of puppies!) you are always looking for something that distinguishes you from the others, and although everyone in my family is very smart, no one had my memory. I walked around so fired up and in perpetual motion (another nickname) that my mother would often say to me, "Mari! Go run around the block a couple of times!" just to get me to burn off some of that excess energy that I was so famous for.

I also loved to mentally take note of everything, because it was my way of having homework just like my two older sisters, who were five and ten grades ahead of me. It gave me a certain power to know that I could spend an entire day "recording" everything for myself, putting it somewhere in my brain, and be certain that I would never lose *any* of it.

My Story of HSAM

Even as a very young child, I began creating exercises and routines that helped me develop my memory. One particular routine began on Saturday, October 24, 1959, the night before I was to receive my First Holy Communion. I was only seven years old and in second grade, but I knew that I was facing the biggest day of my life thus far, and I was so euphoric that I wanted to remember every little feeling I was having before going to sleep. I decided to play a little game with myself, in which I tried to remember every day that had led up to that moment starting with the most recent. *What did I do a week ago? Two weeks ago? Three weeks ago?* I even started to go back to the previous years and the year before that, remembering specific days from first grade and kindergarten.

Over time, this exercise became not only my routine to fall asleep, but also a way to mentally challenge and exercise my brain to the point that I could "time-travel" back to: *What did we do each day of our vacation? What was I doing when I was exactly to the day my younger brother Lorin's age? My niece Lizzy's age?* And it was not just about touching down on a fleeting image or a feeling from the past, but rather going deeper and deeper into memories and specific moments, exploring my past through the lens of the present.

As I grew up, what began as a mental game to challenge myself and relish my First Holy Communion became a nightly routine and a chance to revisit and meditate on my past day, week, year, or decade. Memories became so vivid that they started to feel like little visits to people and places that didn't exist in my life anymore.

This activity was both fascinating and comforting to me. I was thrilled about my ability to do this and assumed most people could do it, as well. It wasn't until I was eighteen that I realized my memory was different. It was during a conversation (on Sunday, May 24, 1970) with my best friend at the time, Ireen Rusniak. While listening to me recall in detail a story from our childhood and my being shocked that she couldn't remember most of it, Ireen stopped me and said, "When are you going to realize that no one else has this crazy memory of yours?" That was the moment when I began taking note of others' ability to recall their past. I realized then that my capacity was different.

From my dorm mates at the University of Chicago, who tested me on the day of the week certain events took place, to an old boyfriend who claimed he lost his past once we broke up, it became common knowledge to my friends and family that I had this baffling memory. Over the years, whenever people wanted to fact-check some event from their lives, I'd get a call asking, "What day was the school picnic three years ago?" "In what hotel in Philly did we stay that time?" "Remember when we went on that boat ride around Manhattan? When was that?" Many years later, researchers would tell me that this ability is called Highly Superior Autobiographical Memory, or HSAM.

Even though the A in HSAM stands for "autobiographical," I still have a strong memory for the usual things. I was a good student, in large part because of my memory, but I do not have a photographic memory or anything like that. My memory is special in its autobiographical detail. I can remember almost every day of my life back to the age of seven (and every day since around twelve) and many incidents and things from my earlier years, all the way back to infancy.

I think it is very common for people to recognize which family members retain memories better than others, because our personal histories are so vital to us. While in some ways, it is no different than the person who can remember every Academy Award winner or the one who can recite baseball statistics, in many more ways, HSAM is very different from these other feats of the mind. Memorizing facts leaves them detached from a personal context. Reciting the dates of battles from the Civil War is very different from conjuring up images of your own past. (Unless, of course, you're a Civil War veteran!)

Scientists have noted that there are three distinct characteristics of people who have HSAM: 1) They tend to spend a greater amount of time recalling their personal history as compared to most people; 2) they have an abnormal ability to remember specific events from their own past more clearly; and 3) perhaps most importantly, HSAMers (as we call ourselves) remember two hundred events or more in the span of any given year, whereas people with average memories generally remember only about eight to eleven. A person with HSAM can describe in intimate detail the events that took place on a particular date; including the day of the week the date landed on, what the weather was like, what they ate for lunch, what they wore, and many more seemingly trivial details. Along with our personal experiences, people with HSAM can also tell you current events that were taking place on that given day, as long as the event crossed our radar screen at the time. We also see all of our memories in the first person, unlike other people, who tend to vary in their perspective. In fact, about 70 percent of all people see their pasts in the third person (à la Scrooge!).

For all these seemingly amazing capabilities, people who have HSAM are not classified as savants or autistic. We are not calendar calculators with a system. For people with HSAM, the knowledge of days and dates is almost built in. We aren't using mnemonic or memory strategies to remember events. When asked how we do it, we all say the same thing: "I just see it! It's just there."

I got to meet my fellow HSAMers on Monday, December 7, 2009, when my good friend Lesley Stahl had arranged to have us all get together for a two-part segment on *60 Minutes*. Lesley has been a friend of mine for twenty-seven years, and on Wednesday, September 20, 2006, she and her producer Shari Finkelstein and I went to lunch. At around that time, *60 Minutes* had been offered the story of Jill Price, the first person to be studied by Dr. James McGaugh, Research Professor of Neurobiology and Behavior at UC Irvine, for her outstanding autobiographical memory. Lesley hadn't been interested in the story, because she didn't think that HSAM (or hyperthymesia, as it was called then) was that rare, having known me for so many years. During this lunch, it was clear that Shari was testing me with dates, but it wasn't until she told me that she had gotten married on June 15, 1998, and I instantly asked her, "Why did you get married on a Monday?" that she knew Lesley was telling her the truth.

Three years later, *60 Minutes* decided to do a bigger story on

HSAM because at that time there were only four more people who had been verified as official HSAMers. Lesley called and asked me to be tested on camera, so there I was—on Thursday, November 5, 2009—put to the test by Dr. McGaugh's team at UC Irvine. After correctly answering over five hundred questions, which included every memory test known to man, as well as hundreds of questions based on current events ("On what day did Princess Diana die?") and my own life ("What was the date and theme of your senior prom?"), I was officially deemed the sixth person with HSAM. I was also given an MRI in order to check out the size and shape of my brain. When four of the other HSAMers (Louise Owen, Bob Petrella, Brad Williams, and the late Rick Baron) and I met the following month, we were not only asked several more questions to illustrate our ability, but we were also genetically tested for motor skills and had to submit samples of saliva.

As an example of how HSAM works, I will explain how I answered one of Dr. McGaugh's first memory questions, "When did Princess Diana die?" I told him, "Well, she actually passed away on Sunday, August 31, 1997, but for me it was Saturday night, August 30. I had just come off stage at the Shubert Theatre where I was performing in *Chicago* and my friend and castmate, MaryAnn Lamb, grabbed me and pulled me into the dressing room where the TV was playing and said, 'There was a terrible car accident in Paris, and Dodi Fayad has died and Princess Diana is hanging on for dear life.' After we watched the TV for a while, a group of us went to Josie's restaurant on Amsterdam and 74th Street, and next to me sat Michael Burresse, next to him his boyfriend Todd, then MaryAnn, Jimmy Borstelmann, my ex-husband Rob who was next to me, and at 12:35 Mary, the maître d', came up to the table over my right shoulder and pulled me away from the table to tell me that Princess Diana had passed away. I went back to tell the others, and we all had a moment of silence. So, to answer your question, it was Sunday, August 31, 1997, but my experience with it was on Saturday, August 30."

What It Feels Like to Remember

On my first day of testing, one of the questions Dr. McGaugh's team asked was, "How does your memory work? For example, when given a date or an event, what happens in your brain that helps you figure out where you were and what you were doing and what day of the week it was? What do you see? Walk us through the process." I laughed to myself because I've been trying to describe my memory process for so long now that I used to start with, "You know how a card catalogue works . . . ?" That progressed to my describing trays of photographs developing side by side, each image becoming more and more vivid as I recall it. This explanation later became, "You know how you can find a scene on a VHS tape by rewinding or fast-forwarding . . . ?" But all of these metaphors were thrown out the window when I first saw the scene selection menu on a DVD. I had found the perfect image. Watching several little movie clips running simultaneously is the closest parallel I can use to explain how I remember, which is unlike many of my fellow HSAMers, who often use the image of calendar pages flipping instead. I see any date I'm asked as though it were placed on a linear timeline, from left to right, January being the far left and December the far right. But it is simultaneous. All the days in a year are there in front of me, and I can choose to hone in on any one, but they are definitely not "on separate pages."

Say, for example, you give me a specific year. The entire year lines up chronologically left to right as though on a timeline, and the easiest days to remember—a major life event from that year or my birthday or Christmas—fill in first. With the whole timeline scrolling through the months and days of that year, my mind then runs through it as though I were watching several movie scenes all at once. If I want to hang out awhile on a particular day, I can zoom in on that day's experience. I can even stop the movie to dwell on a particular moment or image.

This process was put to the test on Monday, December 20, 2010, the day after the *60 Minutes* story on HSAM aired. I was on CBS's *The Early Show,* and the lovely host Rebecca Jarvis gave me the year 1975. This was a year I hadn't scanned through for a very long time, but I immediately saw the left-to-right "timeline" of little video-like scenes, and on it my birthday (Sunday, April 6) and Christmas (Thursday, December 25) came up first. I knew I couldn't stop for very long on the images I was seeing, because it was only a four-minute segment, and I wanted to be good television. I then saw what date Thanksgiving fell on that year (November 27, a Thursday, of course) and what day of the week Valentine's Day was on—Friday in this case. (I guess I organically picked days that illustrated day and date.) And knowing I was running out of time, I quickly mentioned Tuesday, August 12, a first date with an old boy-friend.

When I was explaining the process to Rebecca, I could instantly see those days, and it was as though I were stopping on that day for a second before moving on to other days within that year. The segment ended, but by the time I got to the car ride home—about fifteen minutes after I was first told to think about 1975—I could literally describe *every day* of that year. Some of the days come up in blocks, such as vacations or the weeks of a particular job. And when I go back to any particular day, I am actually there again in first-person perspective looking out through my eyes and reliving the experience as if it were happening for the first time. Because I can do this so easily at this point in my life, I can also more or less visit with a new perspective when I want to go back to a memory and see it with a more recent sensibility. I can revisit an experience with an old boyfriend, for example, and see it through my eyes then, but with a different understanding because of who I am today. Say I go back to my fourteen-year-old self and relive the pain of finding out that I wasn't being asked to a junior ring dance. I can literally be back in that moment and feel the sting of realizing how much more he liked the girl he chose instead of me. But I can also go back and appreciate my feelings, the guy's decision, and be proud of how I handled it at the time. (I can also go back and know that, the following year, he would not only ask me to his senior prom but also try to date me many years later when we were in our thirties!) And even though that teenage rejection is not the same now as an adult, I can relate back to those kinds of moments in the past as a reference, because in some ways, the feelings of rejection never change. It still hurts, but the greater you understand what's going on, the less it stings.

In other words, I can be in these old memories, when I choose to, with a *Peggy Sue Got Married* point of view, as it were. If you remember that film at all, you would remember that Kathleen Turner's forty-three-year-old character gets magically transported back to her life as a teenager and is able to revisit her past as her old high school senior self, armed with the wisdom and twenty/twenty hindsight she has acquired since. She can look at her soon-to-be-husband with the knowledge of what he will become, spend time with the sexy outcast now knowing how special he really was, and help the class nerd discover future inventions. Exercising your autobiographical memory gives you a similar kind of wisdom because you are literally able to go back and visit your past with new understanding and experience (without being able to influence future inventions, of course!).

Better Autobiographical Memory—BAM

Since I was eighteen years old, I have recognized that my memory is highly unusual, and I have seen my brain scans, which, according to Dr. McGaugh, prove that I have "several brain regions which are significantly larger than the average person's. These consist of brain regions known to be involved in memory, including those regions close to the hippocampus and caudate nucleus." I also know that according to Aurora K. R. LePort, one of McGaugh's researchers, "An additional rigorous test, given to confirm the presence of HSAM, was given to Marilu. Ten random dates from throughout her lifetime (age of fifteen to the present time of testing) were selected and she was to give the researcher the day of the week each date fell on, the details of what happened to her on that day and the details of a public event that occurred within a month of that date. Twenty-eight people claiming to have HSAM have been given this test. She, along with only two others, received a perfect score." Someone with HSAM always answers every date question with a personal story.

However, there is no doubt in my mind that my autobiographical memory is a product of both nature *and* nurture. The same skills that I learned from my father and the same exercises and routines that I have used over the years to train my memory can give anyone a Total Memory Makeover and help them develop what I like to call BAM—better autobiographical memory! I know that most memory books focus on improving your memorization skills when it comes to lists and names, but there has never been a book that zeroes in on improving your autobiographical memory. And as someone who has HSAM, I can guide you through your Total Memory Makeover from the inside out. So little has been studied, much less taught, about HSAM, because it has only been a few years since doctors and scientists labeled the condition. I have been teaching memory classes and giving lectures on memory throughout the country for several years now, and the big surprise for me has been how receptive people have been to this way of looking at and remembering their histories.

Throughout this book, I will be giving you a series of exercises to help prompt and access your memory and to teach you how to sharpen your memory skills all through your life. These exercises are designed to improve your autobiographical memory, and I'm sure that if you give yourself over to the process, you will find new ways to access old memories. (If nothing else, you will have an idea of what it's like to have my memory!)

EXERCISE #1: HOW DO YOU SEE MEMORIES?

How do you access your memory?

- Is it similar to the way I remember? Like scene selection on a DVD?
- Do you see random images? Do they appear as if in a dream?
- Activate your memory by using a simple example. Try to recall any activity you engaged in yesterday. Anything is acceptable, but the more vivid the better. Once you lock on to one activity, try to bring back as much from that moment as possible. Notice how those images came to you?
- What did you use to guide yourself to that moment?
- Were there certain triggers, like emotions or smells, or markers, like time of day or specific locations?
- When you revisited that moment, what was your perspective like?
- Did you watch yourself in the activity? Or did you see the activity through your own eyes the way you did when you originally lived it?

Keep your answers to this exercise in mind as we proceed, or even better, jot down a couple of things you've noticed, like "first person" or "smell." This will not only help you later on, it will also be fun to see how you answered the first question of your Total Memory Makeover. The more you understand your own unique process for recall before we start playing with it, the better control you will have as you start to improve and further develop your BAM. Of particular import is the point of view in your memories. Pay attention to this perspective during this and all other exercises throughout this book.

What Is Memory?

The more connections that can be made in the brain, the more integrated the experience is within memory.

—*Donald T. Campbell*

There is nothing more fascinating to me than memory! I love the sheer idea of it, the way it works, its beauty, and its complexity. The more associations you can make through memory, the more rewarding your life will be.

Let us begin with the broadest definition of "memory," because within this will be all of the different and nuanced forms memory can take. According to the dictionary, memory is the process of recalling what has been learned and retained, especially through triggers and repetition. In the words of this definition lie the two most general categories of memory: short-term memory, which is the immediate re-creation of a piece of information, and long-term memory. There is more to memory than rote repetition, and the word "retained" in the previous definition starts us down that road, the road of long-term memory.

Let's look a little closer at these two categories. Have you ever been given a seven-digit phone number, remembered it long enough to dial it, but forgot it the second you heard it was a wrong number? Well, that is your short-term memory working for you. Short-term memory is the storage of information for only a short period of time.

Conversely, have you ever tried to figure out how your partner is able to remember an argument you both had five years ago? Or how your teenager can remember a poem he or she learned back in second grade? That, by contrast, is long-term memory, and it involves the retention and recollection of information over a long period of time, such as days, weeks, years, or even decades.

From the various memory tests I took at UC Irvine, I have learned that there is no one spot in the brain for memory, but rather many different areas of the brain that are used to store different types of memory. This is especially true for long-term memories, for within this group we can make even further groupings and divisions. Under the umbrella of long-term memory are explicit memory, implicit memory, episodic memory, and semantic memory.

Explicit memory, a type of long-term memory that we all share, is the ability to comprehend and remember information consciously. It is what most people have in mind when they think of memory, and it is what you might use when remembering a doctor's appointment or someone's birthday. It is also what a person may use when studying for an exam or any time one needs to make a conscious effort in order to remember the information they are receiving. When I tell you what I was wearing on, let's say, Sunday, May 15, 1977 (bell-bottom jeans and a mint-green T-shirt with capped sleeves), that is an explicit memory that I am consciously recalling.

Implicit memory, on the other hand, does not require conscious thought. This type of memory allows you to do and remember things by repetition. It is where human beings are "mechanical." Implicit memory is information that becomes second nature to you, in the way that driving and the rules of the road become after years of being behind the wheel. These are things that become habit, like brushing your teeth or putting on your shoes. Implicit memory is the *result* of explicit memory. If you practiced very hard for that driving test using explicit memory, the fruits of your labor would manifest in the habit of driving, using implicit memory. I may have sat in bed when I was a little girl and consciously ferreted out what I did the month before in my mind, but at this point, it's literally "just there." The act of remembering, for me, is completely second nature.

There are also various other types of long-term memory that have recently captured researchers' interest, including prospective memory, retrospective memory, emotional memory, and, finally, the focus of this book—autobiographical memory.

Autobiographical memory (AM), another form of long-term memory, is based on an individual's life, and it's the one you're going to improve over the course of this book. With AM, the brain uses episodic memory (personal experiences, specific objects, associated emotions, people and events experienced at a particular time and place) and semantic memory (general knowledge and facts about the world, related to no specific event). For example, an episodic memory would be your happiness at your sister's wedding (on Monday, June 17, 2002, for me at least!) and semantic memory would be your knowing that a bride at a wedding is the one getting married.

The biggest misconception about autobiographical memory is that it is photographic memory, also called eidetic memory, which is the ability to recall images, sounds, or objects after a short time of exposure. In fact, assuming that what I have is photographic memory, people will often ask, "So, you can just read a script once and know all the lines?" The answer to that is no. Although I am very good at memorizing a script quickly, it is not because of my autobiographical memory, but rather because of my explicit memory.

With autobiographical memory, it is more about the experience of what you are doing, where you are doing it, and what is going on around you at the given moment an event is taking place. It can resonate in significant ways, like remembering how you felt when an important life lesson took place. And it can keep that lesson alive long after the incident has passed. It can also help prompt seemingly insignificant connections that can be helpful later. Apropos of the script question, when I read a script, my autobiographical memory allows me to remember not only the script, but where I was when I read it, thus enabling me to remember the lines in a more connected way.

For example, when I first read the script to the musical *Chicago,* it was Monday, March 17, 1997, and they had sent it to me because they were interested in my replacing Ann Reinking in the Broadway production. I hadn't seen the show yet, but I did know two things: that it was a brilliant production, and that to get the job, I would have to work my butt off! I can remember sitting in my bedroom with script in hand and being surprised at how spare and precise the text is. I remember looking up and seeing the teal-green chair in my bedroom as I was thinking how much the character of Roxie was like a little kid (my own boys were both under three at the time) and how the characters were written, at least in this version of the script, without much description, thereby leaving a lot up to interpretation. I can't tell you how many times during my 374 performances I flashed back on that first reading of the script while sitting on my bed to bring myself back to the spare and precise essence of the show. This type of cross-connection between activity and time and place happens numerous times throughout my day, usually in a flash of thought, but significant nonetheless. It is just one more example of how HSAM works.

The following chart will give you an at-a-glance explanation of the different types of memory.

MEMORY CHART

TERM	DEFINITION	EXAMPLE
Short-Term Memory	The recall of information for a relatively short time.	Remembering a seven-digit phone number for a few seconds in order to dial it.
Long-Term Memory	The retention of and ability to recall information over a long period of time, such as days, weeks, years, or even decades.	Remembering a poem you learned in high school or an argument you had with someone a month ago.
Explicit Memory	The ability to comprehend and remember information consciously.	Remembering an appointment, a birthday, a script, or information while studying for a test.
Implicit Memory	Memory that does not require conscious thought. Remembrance through repetition.	Knowing how to drive after driving for many years, or how to brush your teeth once you've learned.
Episodic Memory	Part of autobiographical memory/declarative memory. The memory of things related to autobiographical events.	Remembering particular times and places in detail, including objects, emotions, people, and events from personal experience.
Semantic Memory	Memory of the meaning and understanding of general knowledge and facts about the world. Unrelated to specific experiences and events.	Knowing that a hamster is an animal or a hammer is a tool.

Autobiographical Memory	Memory about specific information in one's life. It is made up of episodic and semantic memory.	Remembering your first kiss, various birthdays, vacations, names of pets/friends/relatives, etc.
Highly Superior Autobiographical Memory (HSAM)	In-depth and detailed autobiographical memory far above the average.	Remembering what you wore, what day of the week it was, what you ate that day, and so on, on any day in your life.
Retrospective Memory	The ability to remember people, words, or events in the past. Can be implicit or explicit.	Remembering your mother's doctor's name or friend's name through passing or purposeful thought.
Sense Memory	Memory recall of physical sensations that were involved in emotional events, not just the emotions themselves.	Being able to recall and "feel" a hot day, a headache, a painful blister, a kiss, a partner's touch, the pain of a rejection, or "taste" a flavor or "smell" a scent.

Tools to Remember: Anticipation, Participation, and Recollection

As explained earlier, my father's dictum—that every event can be broken up into anticipation, participation, and recollection—has guided me through my life and helped me develop my autobiographical memory. Almost unconsciously, the people in my family still automatically relate everything to APR to this day. I think most of us do, even if we don't realize it. We all look ahead to things before we actually do them. No matter what it is—going to the doctor, on a date, to school, or to work we tend to think about an experience before it happens. After we *anticipate* the experience, we then, of course, *participate* in the actual event, followed by its *recollection* of some sort. The APR cycle is the building block of experience and of life itself, but unfortunately, many of us go through these things unconsciously. We don't spend as much time as we should preparing for the events in our life, thinking about what we hope to get out of the experience and how best to get it. We don't actively participate enough and are often distracted or texting during real-life conversations, or we don't take in our surroundings or really listen. Most glaring, though, is how quickly we walk away from something we've just done without any attempt to remember it. For each of us, the more cognizant effort we put into the immediate recollection, the more deeply embedded in our mental hard drive that experience will be, thus improving our long-term memories of the experience.

Let's think about anticipation for a moment, because anticipation is perhaps the most nascent stage we enact. When we are young, we yearn so completely for so many things—our dads to come home from work, summer vacations to start, the holidays to begin—that some of the easiest memories to conjure up are not about the participation in big events, but rather the anticipation of those events. I remember as a child loving the Christmas season and all of its rituals, and how I could not wait for them to start.

> *Even writing these words, I am remembering Wednesday, December 21, 1960. I am eight years old and in third grade, Sister Paula Marie's room, and the Candlelight Ceremony is taking place, where each class gets to perform the Christmas carol they've rehearsed for the event. My class is singing "Away in a Manger," and I am singing loud and with great in-*

tention, because it seems a more grown-up song choice than last year's (second grade's) "Joy to the World," although not as sophisticated as what will be our sixth-grade song, "O Holy Night." I am now flashing on Tuesday, December 10, 1963, and my mother and I are buying three trees, one for our living room and two to set around the pole in the center of our low-ceilinged dance studio, which was then in the basement. (You have no idea how small our house really was!) The whole family made a party out of decorating the house and dance studio each year, and all of this was in anticipation of Christmas Eve and Christmas Day.

We love the feeling that something wonderful is ahead of us. Is it easier to remember the extended excitement of giving the perfect gift or the momentary joy of receiving one, even if it's perfect? Anticipation is very strong, whether positive or negative, and, considered this way, it is obvious that many of our strongest memories come not from the actual events, but rather from our anticipation of and preparation for those events.

For example, why did we anticipate Christmas so feverishly? Because we remembered how great last year's was! The recollection of past events sets the stage for anticipating the next ones. Circling a date in a calendar imprints that date on your mind. Later, it will be easier for you to remember the exact date of some past event, because you spent time anticipating it. A first step to improving our memories is focusing on upcoming events and anticipating their arrival. If we can just slow down enough to see what is coming, we can be better equipped to participate and will have already made the cognitive bed for recollecting. We'll already have strong memories of anticipation before anything actually happens.

Oddly enough, participation is often the least satisfying of these three stages. Is this not the truly pathetic thing about human experience? Whether we like it or not, it's extremely difficult to fully be present in a moment. Only in memory can you hope to discover the full significance of a moment that you didn't fully recognize at the time. The present is elusive. Like a bar of soap, the present is hard to get a grip on, because just as we close in on the present, it becomes the past. It is impossible to analyze except in anticipation or recollection. If we do not fully live in the present, then we will only have memories of anticipation and recollection, never of enjoyment and fulfillment. Our lives hinge on the ballet of these three activities. Imagine the person who lives his or her life solely in anticipation. In the entertainment industry, you meet many people who have no interest in what they're working on right now, because they want to be doing things that are bigger and better. For this reason, they never take full advantage of their current opportunities and never progress. These people are found in every area of life. There are also people who live solely in the past. I'm sure you can think of a few of those, too.

If anything, it's best to live presently, in the moment, because this leads to the other two rather than blocking you off from either one. When we participate actively in our lives and open our senses to all the stimuli around us, we build memories that can be retrieved and enjoyed the rest of our lives. For example, one of my favorite things to do at a party is to help out the host. I like to be in the kitchen, prepare the food, plan the seating, and just be involved! Of course, because I am so engaged, participating so vigorously, I build strong memories to remember the party later. I know who brought the guacamole, who enjoyed the strawberries, who came late, and who did not come at all. We tend to get this involved only when we are doing or feeling something that is important to us. Soon we will discuss your Track and how these times of exceptional involvement lead to those memories that are especially vivid.

Frequent recollection of any of life's moments is the key to attaining a better autobiographical memory. (Practice makes perfect, right?) I know that part of the reason I have such a strong personal memory is because I have spent my entire life instinctively reviewing my past and pasting the memories up against my internal timeline. This timeline has served to keep my memories in a chronological order that allows me to access them at any time, from anywhere in my life. Spurred on by my father's belief that recollection is the best part of any event, I have, from a young age, tried to savor all of my experiences. I have reviewed them time and again, from every angle possible.

I rejoice in recollection, because it allows me to again relive moments that have passed and that will not come again, unless I remember them. Whether this is to remember a moment in the car with my teenage son Joey from last week or a moment with my brother from forty years ago, these recollections are sweet and further build my memories. I live in APR. It doesn't torture me or torment me. It doesn't take long, and it doesn't take me out of my day.

When we spend some part of our day reviewing the previous day, we are more likely to learn from our mistakes, to improve our behavior, to enhance our current day, and to retain what we have learned into the future. If we slow down and "smell the roses," we will also improve our ability to recall each day and how the flowers smelled the day before, or how Mother's bread smelled when we were ten years old!

EXERCISE #2: APR

As a first little step toward mindfully experiencing your life, let's spend a moment examining your current A's, P's, and R's.

- First, what are you currently anticipating in the future? Is there anything happening in the next few days that you are preparing for?
- Next, what are you in the middle of participating in right now? Are you taking full advantage and appreciating that which is presently going on in your life?
- Lastly, what situation or event from the last few days can you strongly recollect as you are sitting there reading this book? Is it something that you would want to remember for years to come?

Memory Lessons

The best case for recollection as the most important component of APR is that it is when our most heightened learning process takes place. It's the time when we step back to look carefully at what we've done—not just the good times, but also the bad and the somewhere-in-the-middle. Because I have reviewed my history regularly like this throughout my life, I can recall thousands of details from my childhood. I can remember every first day of school and what I wore (most memorably a crazy green and orange ensemble on my first day of sixth grade, Wednesday, September 4, 1963!), every teacher, classroom, and where I sat, every birthday and Christmas, including gifts and who gave them to me. And I remember so much more. Even as young as eighteen months old! I still practice my time-travel exercise whenever I have trouble falling asleep or feel like "visiting" any specific day or time in my life, or, especially, when I want to figure out exactly, to the day, what I was doing when I was either of my sons' ages. (One of the most interesting perspectives on my past *ever*!)

I've never found a downside to recalling my memories. Thinking about the good ones has always been enjoyable and rewarding. And visiting bad memories not only allows me to feel grateful that I've gotten past them, but also reminds me what I've learned from those unpleasant and painful experiences. With each "bad" memory comes a major life lesson. It doesn't matter if it's from the time I didn't do my homework in second grade and how mortified I felt at not being prepared, or when I was caught in a lie by a friend while trying to get out of our plans, or even when I found out my first husband had cheated on me. I would go back over these lessons and relive them, so that they became part of me, and I wouldn't make the same mistakes again. To this day, I am vigilant about preparation and homework, am honest with friends, and have stayed away from philanderers.

A good autobiographical memory is also like an insurance policy against loss. It has kept my parents alive in me for so many years. I lost my father when I was seventeen and my mother only nine years later. Losing my parents so young was a terrible experience, but I would rather remember their deaths every day than forget my time with them for even a single day. My ability to recall my parents and all of the details of the life I lived with them keeps them present and with me. We all have this ability not to lose our loved ones, to be able to go back to happier times or to learn something from a past mistake. All of the moments that have made up my life may have been lost if not for my memory, and for this reason, I look at it as a line of defense against meaninglessness. What was the purpose of my fight with my brother in 1968 unless it informed the arguments I'm having with my teenage son in 2011? We all owe it to ourselves as living beings to take full advantage of the wealth of our own experiences.

Nippersink Manor Resort was like the resort in the 1987 film Dirty Dancing, *only instead of the Catskills in New York, it*

*was located in Genoa City, Wisconsin. I remember Wednesday,
July 26, 1967, when I was fifteen and a guest at the resort, and
our nineteen-year-old busboy Sammy and I stayed up most of
the night listening to the soundtrack of* A Man and a Woman
*while getting his wait station ready for breakfast. I couldn't be-
lieve that after Sammy and I had flirted all week, we were now
slow-dancing to sexy grown-up music in the dining room, then
moving on to a poolside lounge chair, where my father found
us at three o'clock in the morning making out. My father, as
you can imagine, was very angry. It was like the scene from*
Dirty Dancing *when Jennifer Grey goes to Jerry Orbach on the
golf course to ask for help. There was nothing but fury and,
worse than that, my father's obvious disappointment in me.
He had been searching all over the resort for me, only to find
me in a compromising position with this cute guy. We walked
back to our guest cottage in total silence. He was furious. But
I couldn't help it; I was so in love with Sammy. I would have
done anything to be with him.*

*The next morning, I found out that Sammy had taken off
with one of the other girls and gone on a road trip. It was a
devastating blow to little fifteen-year-old me. But what I get
from this memory now is not so much Sammy, nor how in love
and then hurt I was when he left, but the memory of my father.*

*I was this young girl on a trip with my family, vacation-
ing at the place I would later work for several summers, and
every time I go to this memory, I have a chance to visit my father again—anger and all. I can see him standing there and
feel my heart jump as he catches Sammy and me making out
on the lounge chair by the pool. I can remember, through my
fifteen-year-old eyes again, seeing my dad. It is intense and it is
sad, but I wouldn't lose this memory for anything in the world.
Why should I? I only had two more years to create memories*

with him—good and bad. I look back on this incident and see how far I have come and how long he has been gone. But for that moment, in that memory of making out with Sammy and being caught, I am that silly, naïve little fifteen-year-old girl again.

And I have my father.

We all have our memories. But yours can be so much deeper, so much fresher, so much richer, if you learn to access your memories and look at them without flinching. I have been giving lectures and teaching classes in autobiographical memory for several years now, and I have witnessed tremendous changes in my students who have improved their autobiographical memories. Together, we have explored the importance of memory and how it helps us layer information and gives us access to things we already know. We have analyzed how an improved autobiographical memory keeps us from starting at square one and becomes the foundation for self-confidence as it builds and develops one's personality. It also becomes easier to size up new situations and see the bigger picture. Exploring your memory is almost like therapy, in that it helps you to better understand yourself and predict how you'll function.

I have my whole life within me, as do you.

Now let's unlock it.

Chapter Two

Your Memory Matters

Memory is the mother of all wisdom.

—Aeschylus

We cannot change our memories, but we can change their meaning and the power they have over us.

—David Seamands

People often ask me, "Isn't it painful to have *your* kind of memory? Isn't it painful to lug around vivid emotional pain from the past? Aren't we better off forgetting *some* things?" I laugh at these questions and, without fail, say, "Not at all!"

Think about the fact that all of your experiences—positive or negative—are stored somewhere in your mind. This becomes obvious when someone, let's say a friend, reminds you of a day or event that you can't remember. The friend insists that you were there, while you insist that you weren't. In your mind, there is simply no possible way that you've completely forgotten this event that your friend so clearly recalls. "You must be thinking of someone else," you say. Maybe your friend starts to tell you details that he or she remembers, like who you were with, what you ate, what the weather was like, and so on, and these elements start to appear before you, in your mind, without significance or relationship. They float in your mind's eye, an amorphous collection of story fragments. And then . . . something happens. Something almost magical, when you think about it. All of a sudden, the location, the people, and the time in your life coalesce, and you begin to connect the dots. "Was that while I was living up on Doheny Drive?" you ask. And your friend says, "Yes! Yes!" And just like that, you've got it. You remember. The whole thing is there, right in front of you. The story's pieces, which only moments previously had no value to you, now have their place in a recalled array. It was in there after all.

You are the result of everything you've experienced. Saying that an unremembered event does not affect your life is also denying that it is still somewhere in your mind, which is untrue. Your amalgamated experiences are what make you a complete and complex person, and even though most of those experiences are forgotten, they still inform you constantly. The things we do not remember can be the keys to understanding why we choose to do the things that we do. If all of these memories are sitting there in your head, and they are subconsciously affecting you in ways worth illuminating, then why do so few of us work toward remembering them? I know firsthand from teaching others to access their autobiographical memories that it is possible to remember a lot more than we think we can. You may not believe now that you can access all that past information, but trust me, it is still in there somewhere—like it or not—and I'm going to show you how to uncover it.

I am, of course, talking about looking back at *all* of your experiences. The truth is, our negative experiences usually contain the most golden insights, but we are so afraid of facing whatever pain could result from reliving them. We are terrified that we may see something that we could have done differently or savored more wholeheartedly and find ourselves plunged into regret. The *fear* of pain, however, is always more searing than the pain itself. We must remember negative events in order to move past them, with the hope of never repeating the choices that made the experience difficult. That's not to say we have to endlessly dwell on the negative, but we do need to accept them for what they are—the past, the stuff of memories, a mental image that has only the amount of power that you ascribe to it. Choosing not to listen to your past, and deciding to leave your memories' influence to the subconscious level, stunts you as a growing, evolving human being. It would be similar to lying to your therapist; you are only cheating yourself. Rather than behaving like "I'll show me!" or falsely telling yourself that you can control your experiences because you can keep pushing them down and repressing them, really come to own your past by recalling it fully. Keep in mind that the better you remember your life, the greater you develop your ability to access the knowledge you've acquired from *all* of your experiences.

This calls to mind the oft-retold fable of the centipede and her legs, a favorite among commencement addressers and self-help gurus. The story goes like this: Mrs. Centipede was walking along with all of her one hundred legs moving in perfect sync. Her sides were undulating waves of little limbs and she was completely mobile. One day, Mr. Cricket saw Mrs. Centipede and wished her good day. They got to talking and everything was going fine when Mr. Cricket said, "You know, I've been wondering, Mrs. Centipede. How do you move so well with all those tiny little legs?"

Mrs. Centipede said, "Golly, Mr. Cricket. I don't know! I've always just walked. I've never once thought about how I move my legs." And as she said that, and started to back away from Mr. Cricket, her legs began to feel foreign. She couldn't remember how she ever controlled all her extremities. Her feet began to cross and her legs became all tangled.

Mr. Cricket began to laugh at Mrs. Centipede, who was now writhing in an attempt to free herself from herself. She just couldn't seem to maintain bodily order like she was so used to doing. After a while, Mr. Cricket left, which made the situation a little bit better, because he was being pretty negative. But even alone, Mrs. Centipede struggled and struggled, finally giving up from desperation, little centipede tears welling up in her centipede eyes.

Finally, in her desperate stillness, one leg twitched and made her aware of it. Thinking about this one leg, she began to move it, slowly at first, then faster. And one by one, she went through all one hundred of her legs, learning how to move each one individually. She became aware of her own body and how she moved, and now that she was conscious of how she moved, she could do backflips and swing from branches, impressing even the cynical Mr. Cricket.

This little story is meant to instruct us that doing things without thinking about them limits us. Freedom to move or to remember comes not from unconsciously relying on instinct, but instead progressing through the interesting work of going leg by leg, year by year, and seeing how and what you can do, what you can remember. This book is partially a guide to becoming more aware of how, what, and why we remember, and understanding those things will allow your mind to do tricks that you never thought it could do.

We've talked a lot about the benefits of dealing with bad memories, but remembering moments of success, of course, is equally important. Noticing and recalling how you made a boss, a teacher, or a client proud and more confident in your abilities is key to establishing a pattern of advancement. What is the easiest way to ensure that someone will continue to excel? By praising them, of course. Why do we give a trophy to every kid on a soccer team? Because we want to encourage them! We want to make their soccer experience special so that they will remember it and learn positive things from it. Seeing that trophy from time to time triggers memories, whether it's the expectation as each of the players was called to the front, or the excitement as the trophy was handed over, or the joy as your teammates cheered for you. These details, if remembered, can greatly influence one's life. These moments are *made* to be remembered! If we don't remember how, where, when, why, and what we've accomplished, how do we keep those accomplishments coming?

Think of life and its many challenges as an enormous maze. At the center, success is waiting, but how do you get there? You need to remember each false start, dead end, and open pathway as you progress, so that you can make successively smarter and better choices. If you don't remember where you've been and what *not* to do as well as what *to* do, you'll keep making the same mistakes and be forced to start over, never making real headway. Likewise, in the maze of real life, your education, career, family, health, and financial and social success all rely on how well you can bring to mind past mistakes and victories—both big and small! It's important to know where the dead ends are, as well as the paths that lead to success; otherwise you are constantly starting over and never really moving forward.

For years, I watched a friend of mine never work for the same people twice, despite his being a brilliant producer and achieving great success for the companies that hired him. He constantly burned bridges because of his attitude on set and failed to take the lesson that he should stop being difficult to work with from one job to the next. He ultimately ended up on everyone's "life's too short" list and had to work outside the country in order to support his family. The new location, however, gave him the opportunity to look at his past behavior and change things around. He is now employed in both countries and has a much happier life, all because he was finally willing to look back to move forward.

Being stuck in one place often leads to a pattern of stagnant or negative behavior, which is easy to repeat again and again when you don't clearly keep in mind the outcome of your actions. But the tendency to repeat bad behavior is more than forgetting consequences; it is not using APR (anticipation, participation, recollection) to its best advantage. It is failing to *anticipate* the end result, so that as you are deciding, for example, whether or not to go ahead and cheat on a spouse, or yell at a child, or lose your temper with a boss, you are forgetting to look ahead at the consequences of your actions. You then *participate* in this self-destructive behavior, and then spend a lifetime trying not to *recollect* all of these painful moments. This desire to escape memories, however, robs you of the chance to change your behavior, as you are not ready to confront your life honestly and change your ways. As a result, you can often repeat the same mistakes over and over again.

For example, as an actor, I learned the hard way that auditions are a great way to learn from past mistakes and improve your chances for getting a job. When you approach each audition armed with the information you've layered from every past audition, you begin to land parts. When I finally made that connection, I got the parts that eventually led to three TV pilots and, finally, to my getting *Taxi*. I began to go to each audition armed with a mental checklist I acquired from past failures. Everything from being late, to being at the wrong place, to having gotten the wrong script or their having changed the character I was auditioning for, to running into my greatest competition or being drenched by the weather—all the things that can go wrong, and often do. If I hadn't armed myself with forethought this way, I would have blindly and repeatedly made the same mistakes. This carrying information forward works for everything you do in life, whether it's job searches, dating, buying a new home, hiring an employee, choosing a doctor or dentist, and so on.

Your personal history is the best road map for your future, but only if you remember it. As I've said, you are the result of everything you've experienced, whether or not you think you can remember it, but before you can retrieve misplaced memories, you may want to consider why they've gone missing.

Selective Memories

"I'll never drink like that again!" We've all heard it. Maybe you've said it to yourself. Some say it only to find themselves binge-drinking the very next weekend. That's because they've conveniently allowed the memory of how they suffered the "morning after" to disappear. They haven't held on to the memory long enough to see the connection between a chance invitation to have a drink after work and the all-night party that followed, or between the few-too-many drinks at the office Christmas party and the embarrassing behavior those drinks unleashed. Then, the next time they're offered that extra drink, they'll take it, because they've forgotten how truly sorry they felt the last time and the promises that they made to themselves.

Forgetting or hiding unpleasant memories may be an unconscious attempt to avoid the shame and pain of them. I know people who have stayed in abusive relationships because they bury their emotional pain along with their memories of the abuse—in the name of survival. They don't realize that their emotional pain could be what pushes them to freedom, if only they'd stop trying to forget it. One friend in particular put up with years of abuse, even leaving her husband at one point after he beat her up so badly she needed twenty stitches in her face, only to go back again and get pregnant with another child. After finally facing the truth of her situation and seeing him for who he is, she left. He tortures her to this day as a deadbeat but overindulgent dad, but at least now she's remarried to a great guy who loves her.

Other people remember the bad times—and only the bad times. They seem to revel in crisis, turning all their memories into melodramas. Remembering only the extremes of emotional experience is just as unhealthy as not remembering at all. Only focusing on the blacks and whites can make you respond in equally extreme ways, whether dramatic, fearful, vengeful, nonresilient, or weak. It might attract attention, but it is definitely not truthful. If you only remember the blacks and whites you'll miss all the grays, and, unless you're Lady Gaga (the epitome of fun extremes!), 95 percent of your life takes place in the grays. Seeing *all* the shades is essential for putting the whole picture into perspective. And perspective is what memory offers.

Accepting and understanding the complete picture creates peace, calm, and understanding, and it keeps you from holding grudges. During the *60 Minutes* shoot, when Lesley Stahl asked the group of us with HSAM whether or not we were grudge holders, a few of us immediately said, "No!" I know that with my memory, if I walked around holding grudges, that would be way too much baggage to carry!

EXERCISE #3: ARE YOU BLOCKING OUT BAD BEHAVIOR?

The goal of this exercise is to be able to identify something that you may be blocking out because you don't want to face the truth of it. This refusal to face something head-on may be holding you back from a more positive life. Is there anything about which you often say, "I'll never do that again!"? When you are once again at the crossroads of the decision whether or not to indulge yourself in that behavior, what is it that makes you "forget" that promise to yourself?

- Is there some strong memory you could conjure up and hold in your mind the next time you start to head in that direction? For example, make a list of all the cons of that behavior (bad for my health, destructive to my career, hurts others, too indulgent, and so on) and all the pros (momentary pleasure, makes me uninhibited, feels good to have a secret, and so on).
- In addition, think of two very specific and illustrative examples of each side to be able to call on the next time you're at the crossroads of a decision.

Greater Emotional Resilience

When you fear your past, you give it power. I'm often asked about bad breakups in one's past, especially by women. They'll say, "Come on, isn't there some guy who broke your heart, and now you don't want to remember and relive that experience?" Yes! Yes, of course I have that in my past. I'm a grown woman with two children, and I have been married three times. Before and in between marriages, I have dated, and my heart has been broken more than once. What woman or man, young or old, hasn't had their heart broken? As for the second part of the question, whether I wish to forget and not relive that experience, no, not really. If you don't reexamine those heartaches once in a while, it is even more disturbing and painful. Life has to be aired out. You have to find the humor and the lesson in everything, even (and maybe *especially*) a breakup. When I look back at every relationship I've had, even my short and tumultuous first marriage, I can see the passion and humor we both had together, and how much I learned about being married from such a bad example of what I would ultimately want. My ex and I (all my exes and I!) are good friends to this day, and I know a lot of it is because my memory has made it possible to refresh the good times and lessons for both of us, thereby making us more understanding and forgiving of one another.

When a relationship ends, a deep emotional impression is left behind. It is very difficult to walk away without spending days, weeks, even years ruminating about what went wrong. Like it or not, this has all the ingredients of what makes a lasting memory: adrenaline, passion, pain, deep thought, and frequent review. Although the source of this experience is pain, a great deal can be learned from all that ruminating and suffering. This is how we grow emotionally. Hopefully, after an experience like that, we have gained a lot of knowledge and experience on this particular subject and can enter the next relationship with much more maturity. The lessons provided by a grieving period can be a good thing, as long as this period doesn't last *too* long. There comes a point where you have to move on. Getting past the negative thoughts and feelings is difficult but important. You have to be willing to look at the situation honestly. Admit to the negative contributions you were responsible for in the relationship, as well as the positive things your former partner contributed.

When we look back honestly at a traumatic experience, we don't just relive the pain; we also relive the lesson. We learn and grow and become stronger. The negative moments from our past help us better appreciate the moments we embraced and enjoyed, in the same way that a blizzard outside helps us better appreciate sitting by a warm fireplace inside.

Facing difficult memories reduces their emotional impact through the natural course of repeated exposure. Revisiting helps you better understand a memory each time you analyze it. Instead of avoiding them, try to think of bad memories with the same appreciation you have when going through an archive box you haven't touched in ten years. Each item that comes out tells a story, and seeing it many years later gives new insight compared to how you understood it when it actually happened. A current perspective gives you a more objective understanding. You begin to clearly recognize why you made certain choices and how you would respond differently to similar circumstances in the future. More often than not, it's a way to conquer what you fear most. There may even be a grieving process as you heal from something you've been holding on to for a while. Allow yourself to feel all of it. If you block yourself off from a feeling, it's just going to rear its ugly head somewhere else. It could even become an "emotional bogeyman." Facing your life's darker moments allows them to wash over you, and afterward you can say to yourself, "Okay, I can pick myself up and move on."

EXERCISE #4: EMOTIONAL BOGEYMEN

In exercise #3, you were asked to look at any bad behavior you might be blocking out because you might not want to give it up. But in this exercise, you are asked to identify something in your life that may be too painful for you to want to look at, in any way.

- Is there a memory that holds such power over you that you don't even allow yourself to remember or even think about it?
- Is it a person? A secret? A time in your life that you feel you have to hide even from yourself?
- What would happen if you completely explored the memory of it for all it's worth?
- What is *your* emotional bogeyman?
- And is it tied at all to the bad behavior you may have uncovered in exercise #3?

The Benefit of Doing Something More Than Once

Tapping into all of your memories is a little like having your picture taken. If you only allow your photo to be taken once in a while, you may be shocked and think, *Is that what I really look like?* But if you have many pictures taken of you, over the course of time, and you consider each one for what it's worth, you will probably discover that most of the pictures are not that alarming. When you do something often enough, the results are put into perspective. With a series of photographs, for example, you can see how your appearance changes with the lighting, the angle of your body, your distance from the lens, or what you were wearing that day. Each of these factors affects the positive or negative outcome of the photo. It's not that you're not photogenic. It's all about the taking of the picture.

If you then take the time to analyze your photos, you'll learn something about the process and start to look at your photographs differently. You'll begin to realize which conditions make you look better than others. And you can set up these conditions in future photos, so that your pictures turn out progressively better.

It is the same thing with your weight. If you weigh yourself more often than once in a while, you discover that your weight fluctuates within a range due to many different reasons (salt intake, time of day, time of the month, travel, and so on). And you can use that insight to make peace with your weight as well as understand and improve upon the conditions that caused an unnecessary panic any particular day.

Perspective is power. With a good autobiographical memory you can gain perspective on your experiences and overcome the negative consequences of them. You can control and even conquer your negative emotions through the use of your memory. There is *always* a story and explanation, especially when so much is riding on one experience.

I remember when a very talented, beautiful teen actress made a small guest appearance on *Evening Shade,* the CBS sitcom I starred in opposite Burt Reynolds in the early nineties. This young actress was flawless in rehearsal but blew two of her five lines during the first take of the live taping. I remember Burt quietly saying to her, "Honey, just relax. Let's take it again, and don't worry, we'll just do it till it's right. There's no rush." Of course, she nailed it on the very next take. I was thinking at the time that it's easy to be smooth when you've got a hundred lines, because you have endless opportunities to redeem yourself if you mess up, but if you've only got five lines, there's a lot more at stake with each line. You've got to nail every one of them. Miss one, and you're down to 80 percent. Miss two, and you're already down to 60 percent. Burt's telling her there was "no rush" probably helped her relax, because she felt she had plenty of opportunities to get it right. It took the weight and focus off each take and each line. That young actress was Hilary Swank, and we all know what she went on to do. She relaxed enough to win *two* Oscars for Best Actress.

All Memories, Great and Small

When I was very young I had an aunt who used to see me reading comic books; she would warn me that the brain only had so much room to store things. She used to say if your brain drawer is full every time you learn something you kick something else out. Be careful—Betty and Veronica might be displacing Shakespeare.

—*Caroline Aaron*

My cousin used to say, "It's true that whenever you learn something new, you have to forget something old. When I learned how to brew my own beer, I forgot how to walk." This is a common subject of jokes, but it is obviously not true. In fact, the opposite is true. The more you learn and remember, the more opportunities new information has to make a memory connection. As we've discussed earlier, learning and remembering something new requires a connection to similar information already in our long-term memory—the human hard drive. This is why teachers often use analogies; the information they want students to remember connects quickly with something they already know. Simply put, the more you remember, the more you become capable of remembering. Who do you think would remember more after reading a book about the latest breakthroughs in brain surgery, a college student majoring in art history or a doctor who has devoted the last thirty years of his life to brain surgery? Using the "brain gets full" logic, the brain surgeon would have too much information on the subject of brains to efficiently take in much more. Obviously the brain surgeon would remember a great deal more from that book than the art history student, because of all the relevant information already in his long-term memory. Have you ever noticed that musicians who already play four or five instruments can quickly learn to play a fifth or sixth instrument? They can certainly develop the skill much faster than someone who starts with a clean slate of no musical skill or memory. It is nearly impossible to accurately calculate the capacity of the human brain. Some estimates are as high as one thousand terabytes, which is more storage space than the entire contents of the Library of Congress. Even though we don't know the precise limit of the human brain, we can be certain that only a tiny percentage is ever actually "filled up."

Don't ever think of your memory as something that gets stressed, full, or overloaded. The more you pack into your brain, the more efficient it becomes at handling big loads. And it better be, because autobiographical memory is not just concerned with the extreme or typically "memorable" events. It captures the ordinary, daily events of our lives—the moments that reveal the nuances and tell the *real* story. The more of them we can remember, the richer our lives will feel.

(Natural) Memory Highs

Google, iPads, iPhones, Droids . . . We have so many memory aids these days, we're all getting a little lazy. Our memories are weaker, because we are no longer using them regularly. And yet, our bodies are still wired for memory, and the wiring goes directly through our emotions.

All memories are not created equal. Some stay with us forever, and others are gone in a flash. Adrenaline has a lot to do with this. Before he began studying Highly Superior Autobiographical Memory, Dr. James McGaugh headed the research that proved memory is tied to adrenaline. Using laboratory rats, Dr. McGaugh's studies uncovered the relationship between the two. His experiments began by placing a rat in a large water-filled tank. In the middle of the tank was a platform hidden just beneath the surface, where the rat could stand or sit as a resting place without having to swim. When the rat entered the tank from the edge, it would swim around for a while until, finally, swimming to the middle, where it would find the desired, hidden platform. This exercise was repeated each day, and as a result, the rat was able to find the platform a little more quickly each time. In phase two, the rat was given a shot of adrenaline right after finding the platform. When the rat was placed in the tank the next day, it went directly to the platform without having to swim around—much faster than the rat without the adrenaline shot.

Human memories benefit from adrenaline as well. Experiences

that excite our emotions will automatically get embedded in our memory. For example, most people can tell you exactly what they were doing when the Twin Towers fell on Tuesday, September 11, 2001, because that event raised our adrenaline. For the same reason, we remember days that mean a lot to us and get our blood flowing, regardless of if it was a positive experience, like the birth of a child or a wedding day, or a negative one, like the death of a loved one.

As memory is tied to passionate experiences, for us mothers, it's easy to remember more events about our children because we are so tuned in to our children and their needs. Our participation in their lives is so all-encompassing that most mothers can give details about the first day their child crawled, walked, fell, talked, or got injured. We remember those particular moments most because they are filled with adrenaline, positive and negative, and we constantly relive them. They are so important to us, and we are usually frequently recalling them for other people, anyway. But, like everything in our memory, if we don't recall these events once in a while we forget the specifics. A unique characteristic of parents, especially moms, is that they have the ability to remember even the common events in their children's lives, mostly because, to the parents themselves, these events are *not* common. They are only common to everyone else.

Another example of experiences that often get seared into our memories are those revolving around dating and romance. These include the first crush, the nervous anticipation of a first date, the progression from infatuation to love, the breakups, the heartaches, all of the things people feel as they search for love. Most women will remember, even months or years later, exactly how their date looked when he arrived, what she wore, what he wore, the perfume, what was said, what they did, and the places they went. Men tend to remember the sexual aspects of those first few connections: her body when he first saw her undressed, how soft it felt, how he felt when she touched him, and how beautiful she looked. Women also tend to keep mementos from those first dates. They'll keep letters, cards, rose petals, and just about anything their date gave them, and this continues to reinforce the memory.

We all remember the first time, and there is no need to answer the question "The 'first time' for what?" What makes us remember that first time? Or are there many first times that just naturally become the touchstones of our memories, the portals to our past? The first time we went to school, or rode a school bus, or went to the movies without our parents—these are events that somehow take a front seat in our mental auditorium of memories. The first driver's license, the first kiss, the first job—these are big events in one's life and they make a huge impression on people's memories. One reason that we seem to remember so much more of our lives from age ten to twenty than we do from thirty to forty is that we experience so many firsts in those ten fateful years. You truly become the person that you will be as you leave your teen years and transition into a young adult. And to be a complete adult, one needs an autobiographical memory, so that the experiences gained can lead to more successful behavior in the future.

Memory is, among other things, like a muscle that needs to be warmed up before you really use it. Going back into your memories is not easy, and it is a skill and an exercise that must be prepared for each day. One way to prepare is to develop small skills like keeping a calendar, filling in a planner, working harder in general to keep up with dates and appointments and whatever from your daily life. In the coming chapters we will talk about these techniques and how best to use them. These clerical skills will help you develop your brain muscle and also teach you useful habits for staying organized. As you learn to open up to your memories you will want to visit them more and more, reinforcing your memory process like a well-trained athlete would their skills. One of the first steps in your Total Memory Makeover is getting yourself primed to remember. Just as an actor prepares for a role, we too must prepare for this journey within ourselves.

Chapter Three

Coming to Your Sense (Memories)

You cannot use everyone else's feelings, or made-up feelings. They always come from you. So you will always be playing yourself, "but it will be in an infinite variety of combinations of objectives, and given circumstances which you have prepared for your part, and which have been smelted in the furnace of your emotion memory." You can only play parts well that you have the appropriate feelings for.

—*Constantin Stanislavski*

There is no doubt in my mind that one of the main reasons I have relished my particular memory and have, in fact, developed it with gusto is because I'm an actor. A superior autobiographical memory is a great asset for an actor, as it allows you to recall experiences and emotions from your past that can inform and flesh out the characters that you are called upon to play. As an actor, you are trained to record all of your experiences and feelings in order to build an extensive library of emotions from which to draw. It is essential to have those emotions available, so that you can then find any character within yourself. This is especially true if the character is very different from you. Deeper emotional resources, therefore, are needed to build that bridge between yourself and your character. Great acting comes not from acting like you *think* the character should act; it comes from finding that character's behavior inside of yourself. We are not always capable of some behaviors (thank God!); however, every one of us is capable of getting into the mind-set that causes any kind of behavior. In other words, you don't have to be a murderer to play a murderer; you only have to imagine outrageous-enough circumstances in your own life that could cause you to think and behave that way. The goal is to become the character, rather than just "act like" the character. For example, when playing a drunk, sick, or nervous character, it's a mistake to act only those qualities, because typically sick people are constantly trying to feel better, drunk people are trying their best to act sober, and nervous people are trying to act relaxed. Their objective is the opposite of what their reality is.

> To be a character who feels a deep emotion, one must go into the memory's vault and mix in a sad memory from one's own life.
>
> —*Sir Albert Finney*

Friday, November 4, 1988, was my first performance in *Carnal Knowledge,* a play by Jules Feiffer that first gained recognition as a movie. I played the role of Bobbie Templeton, a depressed, suicidal soul originally played by Ann-Margret in an Academy Award–nominated performance. This was a difficult character for me to play, because, despite the fact that I looked like the character physically, I have never, in my entire life, been suicidal, or anything close to it. I knew it was going to take a lot of what actors call "sense-memory work" to bring me to that emotional state of mind every night. So I filled my dressing room with music that reminded me of bad breakups and a special handwritten letter from my mother who had passed away ten years before, and I also kept a bottle of cologne worn by an unrequited love. Night after night, I brought in anything I could to stimulate profound and heartfelt memories from my past. This sense-memory exercise, which I'd learned years before in acting class, was the only way I could prepare each night for that role.

I originally learned to record and store my emotions as a strategy for acting, but I quickly learned that this was closely tied to my constant recording and remembering. When I could remember the intense emotionality of anything, it became much easier to remember it in great detail. It is also great for understanding human behavior, personal life coaching, and sound decision-making. The more you identify with a multitude of emotions, the more you understand yourself and the people around you. This is essentially the theme of this book—that knowing oneself through recalling your memories is the most powerful tool you have to effect positive life changes, as it allows you to access all of your experiences and to relearn lessons that may have been consciously forgotten. It is vital, therefore, to understand and use the idea of sense memory and emotional memory even if you have no interest in acting.

Sense memory, though specifically valuable to an actor, can be used by any of us in our daily lives—the teacher who needs to empathize with a student, the boss who needs to understand so he can motivate his employees, the parent who needs to remember his feelings as a child so that he can relate better to his own children. Our sensory receptors are our connection to the world around us, and they function in our brains like portals both to our emotions and to our past. Proust knew this when he wrote about madeleines in *Remembrance of Things Past*. And Aristotle was aware of it more than two millennia earlier when he wrote, "Nothing is understood by the intellect which is not first perceived by the senses."

Memory and the Five Senses

All we have to open the past are the five senses . . . and memory.

—*Louise Bourgeois*

Which of your five senses are you most connected to? Which one excites and inspires you the most? Do you dance out of bed because you hear a beautiful classical piece on your iPod or clock radio? Are you motivated to face your day by how the early rising sun paints the landscape outside your bedroom window? Or do you wake up energized by the smell of freshly brewing coffee? Just as some people are stimulated by words (writers, poets, and comedians) and other people are strongly connected to numbers (mathematicians, options traders, and accountants), people can be divided by which of the senses they are most acutely connected to. This is not always easy to determine in oneself, but it's often quite noticeable in our friends. Have you ever attended a gathering where the house décor and party decorations are exquisite and impeccable, but the food is forgettable? (Or worse, memorable because it was so bad?) You could surmise that the host has a strong visual sense but may be less focused on their sense of taste or smell. Or have you taken a ride with a friend whose car seems to be just an excuse for their stereo, a rolling entertainment center? Such a person is probably very sensitive to sound, but not nearly as tuned in to his other senses.

Stimulating any of your senses can trigger a flood of memories, but that is especially true for your strongest sense, which can also tell you a lot about who you are. Many consider it a way to distinguish your personality type, similar to zodiac signs. Knowing your strongest sense helps explain what is most important to you and what types of moments and experiences you are most likely to re member.

EXERCISE #5: WHAT IS YOUR STRONGEST SENSE?

Here is a quiz that the people at Marilu.com have had a lot of fun with, as it helps you determine which of the five senses is your most dominant followed by a description of your "sense" personality type. Almost every person who has taken this quiz agrees with the results.

To begin, number a paper from one to ten. Answer with the corresponding letter for each question. Remember to move quickly and don't get stuck too long on one question. This shouldn't take you more than a couple of minutes.

1. Which appeals to you most?
    a. Corn
    b. Lilac
    c. Calla lilies
    d. Cactus
    e. Mango

2. Which is your favorite thing to do on a day off?
    a. Go to a movie
    b. Spend the day at the beach
    c. Visit a museum
    d. Participate in sports
    e. Dine at your favorite restaurant

3. Which of these are you most likely to collect?
    a. Records or CDs
    b. Antique books

c. Art and design books

d. Travel or nature books

e. Cookbooks

4. Which is your favorite part of a wedding?

a. Dancing

b. Open bar

c. The ceremony

d. Visiting with friends

e. The food

5. What do you enjoy most about school?

a. Socializing with friends

b. The feeling of fall in the air

c. Learning new information

d. Buying new pencils and supplies

e. The cafeteria

6. Which of the following frightens you most?

a. Violence

b. Fire

c. Loneliness

d. Floods

e. Famine

7. Which one of these colors appeals to you most?

a. Black

b. Orange

c. Red

d. Rust

e. Yellow

8. Which of these guides you most?
    a. A Higher Power
    b. Passion
    c. Logic
    d. The advice of others
    e. Instinct

9. Which of these is your favorite part of a romantic evening?
    a. The right music
    b. Foreplay
    c. The way your partner looks
    d. Holding hands
    e. An intimate dinner

10. Which among these is your favorite holiday?
    a. Independence Day
    b. Christmas
    c. Halloween
    d. Valentine's Day
    e. Thanksgiving

Now add up how many of each letter you answered. The letter you answered most often is the sense you are most connected to.

    a. Sound
    b. Smell
    c. Sight
    d. Touch
    e. Taste

Tabulate your answers like these examples. The following scores are mine and Lorin's, showing our orders of dominance for our five senses:

Mine
4—B's: Smell
3—A's: Sound
1—C: Sight
1—D: Touch
1—E: Taste

Lorin's
4—C's: Sight
2—A's: Sound
2—D's: Touch
1—B: Smell
1—E: Taste

Sound

When you are most connected to your sense of sound, you often find yourself at live concerts, listening to music at home, or closing your eyes during a nature walk to take in your surroundings. You especially enjoy listening with headphones, so you can focus and isolate the subtleties within each piece of music. When a rainstorm breaks out, you immediately open the windows to hear the raindrops. Sound people are thinkers and dreamers. They have no trouble spending quality time by themselves, yet they are highly sought after for friendship, because they are great listeners and sensitive to tone, which others appreciate. Sound people tend to be detail oriented. They rarely rush through projects at work and would rather hear verbal instructions than receive visual directions. Sound is the sense that brings the rhythms and the beat into our bodies. We respond so quickly and emotionally to music, poetry, and rhetoric that we don't even notice how much we retrieve our past to entertain our present. Old songs are one sure way to find a track into your memories; they evoke something so basic in us that making connections to our past is easier and faster.

Smell

When your sense of smell is your strongest, you may often find yourself shopping for candles or in bath shops trying all the different lotions and perfumes. You associate each holiday with its particular aroma, and one of your favorite parts is how wonderful the house smells from the cooking. You would never buy a fake Christmas tree, less for aesthetic reasons than because you'd miss the fresh scent of pine. Scent people can identify anyone by their smell and tend to choose a few close friends for life over lots of friends that come and go. In an intimate relationship, there is no bigger turn-on than how your partner smells. And if that strong chemical reaction isn't there, the relationship will go nowhere. (Owning up to firsthand experience on that one!) Like the taster, scent people love to cook, the more aromatic the better. But unlike tasters, who are more hands-on with their cooking and make adjustments based on taste, aroma folks love to periodically check back in and out of the kitchen to "nose" any changes in their progress. People whose sense of smell is their strongest are more likely to have better memories than sight or sound people. The olfactory cortex is very near to both the brain's memory center (the hippocampus) and the brain's emotion center (the amygdala), which is why a smell can spark a memory even more quickly and intensely than a photo or song. It has even been proven that learning is enhanced when accompanied by a strong smell. The strength of our sense of smell is amazing—we can pick up a scent from mere particles of dust floating through the air! People pamper their noses, cover them up, and spray chemicals into the air to "freshen" it. Smell is there precisely to "sniff out" the corrupt and nefarious. The man who can "smell the coffee" cannot be fooled. When we encounter a smell from our childhood, it can transport us back in an instant. Our ability to recall different smells is a direct link to our subconscious and, therefore, our deepest memories.

Sight

When sight is your most dominant sense, you tend to make choices based on how they appeal to you visually, whether it's travel, art, locations, or architecture. You sometimes choose your hotel rooms based solely on the view and are happiest sipping a glass of wine from a train window. You are often told that you think too much. Sight people also tend to be analytical and inwardly focused. Sight is most often considered the king of the senses. When we are seeing something beautiful the other senses fall away. But it seems to be the most vulnerable, as well, and the dread of blindness is universal. People who are very visual favor their eyes to bring in the world. They "don't believe it until they see it"; they "walk with their eyes open." Most of us think of our memories visually, but just think how fantastic it is that we can imagine in our minds what our eyes can see in the outside world. What gave us such great power? Who needs a television set? Whether in dreams or in memories, our ability to "see" these things is a testament to the strength of our brains and the untapped powers within.

Touch

If your sense of touch is highly sensitive, you probably find yourself choosing sheets and towels based on thread count and cotton quality rather than color, pattern, or price. Warm rainstorms are appealing to you, but never from inside your house looking out through the window. You like to be out dancing in the middle of it with and without an umbrella à la Gene Kelly. You have a very difficult time resisting the urge when the sign says, "Do Not Touch!" Touchers also tend to care a great deal for other people and are deeply hurt when someone betrays them. Perhaps the most generous of all the sense types, touchers make great healers, lovers, and massage therapists, of course. The first sense to develop is touch, and it is ever present and multidimensional in a way that the other senses are not. Is touch present in a dream or a memory? Or does touch, like a jolt in the night, wake you from a dream or a memory? I know that I have dreamed that I was touching, though the feel of the touch was not quite there like the sights and sounds of my dreams. Do we remember how it feels to touch? Is it a more elusive memory than a sunset or a smile? For all of us, there awaits the potential to develop and remember more about our sense of touch.

Taste

When taste is your dominant sense, you may find yourself hosting dinner parties, because tasters naturally make great chefs! This also tends to make them very sociable. Very good at describing flavors, tasters can pick out the subtle ones everyone else misses in glasses of wine: asparagus, nutmeg, bell pepper, artichoke, grass, biscuit, earth, hay, kerosene, figs, and wet wool. Tasters are very close cousins to sniffers. Both can also be offended by bad, subtle odors and flavors. Tasters are often the center of attention. They are perhaps the most gregarious of the sense categories and live every day to the fullest. They *eat* life! We can all only taste sweet, sour, salty, and bitter, and with these four tastes we can discern what water is drinkable, what fruit is ripe, what food has gone bad, or what wine has turned. Taste in this sense is a great monitor for health, and thus for survival. It is a sense that is very strong and helps memories linger. Like touch, how we remember taste is elusive, but the memories are there.

Activating Your Senses

Now that you have a better understanding of the significance of your five senses, let's find an object for each sense to "play" with. We broke it down this way once in one of my acting classes, and it helped tremendously. Each week, we focused on a different sense—"If it's week three, it must be aroma day." Do this yourself with actual objects. If it's not practical to go searching around your house right now, you can also just use objects right near you. For example, if you are reading this on a plane or train, you can use peanuts for smell or taste, your iPod for sound, and the upholstery on your armrest for touch. (Be careful. You don't want to accidentally use the arm of the person sitting next to you or the flight attendant. Save him or her for the visual!) To elicit the deepest, most profound memories, this exercise works best with objects with which you have a strong connection. You will see, however, how well this works even with something as basic as a cocktail napkin. Let's begin.

EXERCISE #6: WHEN IN AROMA . . .

It's Acting/Memory 101, and we are going to start with your sense of smell, your olfactory sense.

- Find a scent that will elicit a strong memory for you—an ex-girlfriend's perfume, a boyfriend's cologne, your father's aftershave, a cinnamon bun, buttered popcorn, a glass of beer, burnt toast, vanilla extract, shampoo, hairspray, deodorant, a cedar closet, a can of dog food, a leather jacket, or an antique book. Even a rubber band might do the job.

- Once you have selected your object, close your eyes and bring the object close to your nose to take a strong, slow, and steady whiff. You may need to scratch, rub, or shake your object beforehand to release more molecules in the air and intensify its scent. It also helps to open your mouth as you inhale through your nose to allow more air to flow through. Your mouth and taste buds are connected to your nose and sense of smell, so this will increase the aroma.
- As you smell your object, think about the very first time you were introduced to this scent. Was it the moment you were expecting?
- Does this scent remind you of any particular person, place, or thing?
- Does it make you happy, sad, angry, sexy, anxious, sleepy, or any of the other seven dwarfs?
- What are some of the visuals you get from this scent?
- Can you step inside the images this scent elicits and connect it to something else?
- You don't have to stop here. Allow your imagination to take you anywhere it's willing to go. Don't rush this. Enjoy the journey. Pay attention to the power one simple scent has over your imagination, psyche, and memory.

When you feel satisfied with what you have learned from your scent object, move on to your next sense and next object. Select some kind of sound sample that stimulates your auditory sense. Find a piece of music, a voice recording, a baby laughing or crying, a train whistling, a musical instrument, or even a can opener.

If you are online, you can find practically anything to listen to, including the most obscure sounds on the planet—whale songs or the latest Björk CD. While listening to your auditory piece, go through the same list you went through with your scent object—who, what, when, where, why, and how is this sound connected to you?

After your auditory object, do the same for your sense of touch. This one could be a cashmere sweater, a silk tie, hand lotion, a pumice stone, or a massage given or received from your partner. If you're giving, don't tell them why you're doing it. As long as you're making the effort, you might as well get full credit for the good deed. Your partner will be so pleased that you were extra-attentive today. Only you have to know that you're doing a sense-memory exercise.

For your sense of taste, I suggest picking something you haven't tasted for a long time, perhaps something from your childhood—a crisp apple, a sweet watermelon, movie-house popcorn. These foods elicit strong feelings from the past. It's fun to taste something you haven't experienced for several years. It's very familiar, and yet, it almost always surprises you in some way, especially if your palate has improved.

After taste, finish off with your sense of sight. This could really be anything and everything. Every object in your house could work for this; however, for the first time, I recommend using a photo. A photo has the potential to bring up so much more than a non-image object can. Don't use a whole photo album. Limit this to just one significant photo, so you can really concentrate and be specific. You may be surprised at how much one photo can conjure up if you try hard enough.

When you're finished with all five senses, take one last moment to review and think about what you've just experienced. Which of your five senses was the strongest during the exercise? Which was your weakest? My strongest is definitely my sense of smell, and my auditory sense is a very close second. My husband has a weak sense of smell but is very strong visually. Once you know your strongest sense, you can lead with it as your go-to sense when trying to unlock a memory that may be deep and difficult to uncover. After identifying your weaker senses, I suggest you exert more effort to exercise them. Learn how to use and strengthen them.

Finally, think about the power of your senses and how strongly they are connected to your memory. Keep this in mind for the rest of the day, and try to remind yourself of this a few times tomorrow, too. Eventually you'll raise your everyday awareness of your five senses and in turn raise your memory receptors for all of your experiences, too. Make every day memorable.

Sense Memory

Now that you've discovered the power of your senses, and before we focus on a specific sense memory, here is a brief explanation of why your five senses (sight, sound, touch, smell, and taste) are information gatherers. Your brain is your command center and storage unit, and your senses are your brain's suppliers. Each sense receptor is designed for the particular stimulus it receives, translates, and transmits as electrical signals, the language of our nervous system, for our brain to understand and process. Sight receptors work by interpreting light collected by the retina. Smell and taste work by chemical interpretation by the nerve cells of our olfactory system and the taste-receptor clusters (taste buds) on our tongues. Sound interpretation is based on vibrations against our eardrums. And touch (the somatosensory system) involves thermoreceptors for temperature, nocireceptors for pain, and mechanoreceptors for pressure and distortion. The reason our senses have such a strong connection to memory is because the light, vibration, chemical, temperature, movement, and pain signals are "recorded" in our sensory receptors.

When we experience sensory stimulus, we naturally return to sensations recorded previously. When we smell a freshly peeled mango, that particular chemical combination is reenacted in our olfactory system, and it is compared to other occasions when we've smelled fresh mango. We are then briefly transported back to one or more of those moments. The same is true when we hear a song that means something to us or has a specific connection to our past. Through this amazing system, a simple scent can take us right back to an exotic vacation, our parents' living room, an autumn barbecue, a childhood sweetheart, fishing with Grandpa, the beginning of an exciting romance, the barracks at our summer camp, a mildewed attic chest or basement cedar closet. And that's just *one* of our five senses!

Electronic technology records two types of sensory information—what we've seen and what we've heard. When we replay something digitally, it can feel as if we are reliving the experience. Imagine how exciting it would be if we could record scents, textures, and tastes in addition to audio and visuals. That would definitely be the biggest hit at the Consumer Electronics Show! We obviously can't videotape every minute of our lives, but when we fully use and appreciate all of our senses, it can feel as if we have.

The aim of sense memory is to prime this process by using an object, image, sound, song, smell, flavor, or texture to trigger the senses and elicit a particular emotional response. For example, when developing my character Bobbie for *Carnal Knowledge*, that sweet letter from my mom put me into an intense emotional state. Even thinking about it now can make me tear up. My mother rarely wrote letters, and this one was very thoughtful and from her heart. Just seeing her handwriting made me sad and gave me an overwhelming feeling of loss. This was appropriate for Bobbie's character, because her essence was that of a depressed, lost soul. The play also takes place in the early sixties, which was definitely my mother's era. Thinking about her automatically places me in that time period. Obviously you can use your senses to remember the best moments of your life as well. What is important is that you explore the way in which certain sensory stimuli can call up memories.

EXERCISE #7: SENSE MEMORY

Exploring sense memory is a powerful memory technique, and it has always been one my favorites in any acting class. Sense-memory work places you in the proper state of mind to experience a particular feeling or emotion. In this exercise, I am trying to help prompt your memories, which will ultimately teach you how to use your current life to access your past. When you use something that has a powerful effect on you, memories come rushing back.

- Choose an object that inspires you to remember something long forgotten. The idea is to "spend time" with this sense-memory object, by either thinking of it, looking at it, listening to it, smelling it, touching it, or tasting it.
- And then leave yourself open to what happens to you emotionally or psychologically.

If you feel as if you have a lot of sense-memory objects and you don't know which one to focus on, don't worry about it. It doesn't matter which one you choose at first; others will start flooding into your awareness. Sense memories happen throughout your day, without your even realizing it. The object of this exercise is not to pick one sense-memory object and then put it away. It is to make you aware that everything in your life is flooded with memories, and these memories are readily available to help put you in whatever mood you need to be in at any given time. You can start to think of your memories as something you can look up, like something on Wikipedia, rather than random images that are called to mind by your environment.

The more you do sense-memory exercises, the more you develop your ability to size up circumstances and instantly know how they will affect you. I have used sense memory in my seminars and on-line classes, not only for curbing food and other addictive cravings like smoking and drinking, but also for helping people get past their issues with self-sabotage and other destructive behaviors. Sense-memory exercises help you remember the adverse feelings you experience as a consequence of reacting negatively to others or from overindulging in food, alcohol, caffeine, or nicotine. Sense memory will help you understand your cravings and negative responses and train you to overcome them. The different influences that affect you are like little magnets attached to your psyche; they will always be part of you. These influences are the essential ingredients that made you who you are today. Let them work *for* you, not against you. Embrace and understand them.

The goal of these exercises is to understand where your emotions are coming from and to be able to feel them without losing control. As you tap into memories and begin to layer your past experiences, you become better at sizing up people and circumstances. You should begin to understand what drives people to do what they do and illuminate others' motivations, not just your own. If, for example, you are able to evaluate a heated situation with a loved one before it gets too hot, you may save yourself a lot of trouble by pulling back and asking yourself, *If I lose it over this issue, what's going to happen? How can I be a more effective communicator so that my point is heard without devastating the other person?* Feeling your feelings, getting overly emotional about them, and then losing all control will only kill your cause. (Who wants to watch that performance, anyway?) If you can find a better way to get your point across so that your "audience" (husband/wife/kids/boss) can hear you, then you'll be much more effective in your daily life. You can receive some much-needed discipline by drawing on the success of such restraint in the past. Otherwise you're always putting your feelings into action, and if we all did that, the world would be a mess. (And most husbands would be dead! Cue music for "Cell Block Tango" from *Chicago!*) Of course, remaining emotionally available without losing control or being overwhelmed by your memories and reactions takes practice, so look for opportunities to practice the sense-memory exercise in different situations in your daily life.

When I say "sense-memory exercise" I mean that you are using something you're sensing and making note of what that calls to mind in your memory. I do this constantly, and if you do, too, then you will make serious strides toward developing your memory. Any time you are reminded of something, go deeper and deeper, and when you see an opportunity to reexperience something that you associate with a past event don't pass it up. Basically I am saying that my memory is good because I love remembering so much, and the more you enjoy having your past called to mind, the more of it you will remember. I encourage you to use these sense memories fearlessly.

EXERCISE #8: SENSE MEMORIES IN ACTION

Think about someone or something in your life you're about to confront.

- What would make you a more effective participant in that situation? Being calm? Fired up? More loving?
- Now, what sense-memory object would help you get into that state of being?
- Choose something that evokes a strong memory to elicit the most appropriate response. For example, before asking for a raise, you might look at a snow globe from your childhood to calm and center you. Or hold your old football trophy before embarking on a new exercise regime. Or look at a "happier times" photo of you and your ex before engaging in a conversation with them about swapping weekends with the kids. You may even listen to the theme song from *Rocky* for all of the above! Whatever it takes to stimulate your memories to make you feel like you can get the job done!

At one point during the course of my memory classes I always ask my students to bring in something (a photo, an article of clothing, a piece of music, etc.) that is connected to a turning point in their lives. During one of these classes a woman brought in a perfume bottle, and there was an entire story connected to this one object. It was the story of a breakup three years earlier that was so bad she practically stopped living. The bottle of perfume was one that she wore throughout the relationship and stopped wearing the day they broke up. It wasn't just that she couldn't wear the perfume; for the past three years she couldn't even look at the bottle or, of course, at any pictures of him. She was paralyzed at that point in her life and didn't know how to get out of the downward spiral she was in. She had gained a lot of weight and hadn't gone on a date since the breakup. The memory class had come at the right time, and she was now ready to face her painful memories head on. She came to realize that blocking these memories was what was keeping her from completely exploring the entire panorama of the relation-ship, including who was responsible for what happened, and why. As a result, she got in touch with her ex and experienced enough closure to get back on track, feel good about herself, get in shape, and begin living her life again. She not only resumed dating, she started wearing the perfume again. Things changed for her as a result of bringing that little bottle into class. She was able to look back at her old relationship for what it was. She took the memories that resulted from the perfume bottle and was now able to move forward.

But it's not just your mind that gets involved in sense memories. Your whole being gets a call to action when dealing with the senses.

Flexing Your Muscle Memory (Move It or Lose It)

Have you ever wondered how you are able to perform physical tasks without thinking about them? How is it possible that we brush our teeth, type an e-mail, or scratch an itch without consciously telling our body parts how to move? Fluid, unconscious mobility is a result of repetition and muscle memory. Put another way, muscle memory is our body's ability to learn and remember through repetitive physi-cal action, but this comes only after an initial phase of conscious and deliberate thought. Learning to walk, crawl, ride a bike, and play the violin is possible because of muscle memory, all of which began with a period of careful, deliberate instruction. Beginning with our first breath, every part of our body is in a constant state of training, learning, and retaining.

The "memory" of muscle memory is not stored in the muscles, as the name implies; it is stored in a part of the brain that can be accessed often and at lightning speeds, similar to the cache in computer processors, which stores the tasks you do most often in the closest, most accessible part of the central processing unit. The more you practice something (practice makes perfect), the more you build that particular type of procedural memory, so your brain can instantly instruct your muscles. The areas where we store muscle memory, the cerebellum and basal ganglia, are connected to higher thinking and motor coordination. The cerebellum is also where motor functions and cognitive learning, like language, are refined. The basal ganglia are located toward the center of the brain and are a part of the system that allows us to form habits. These parts of the brain work together to form the subconscious information that is muscle memory.

We can see the benefits of developing muscle memory in many skills; an obvious example of this is proficiency in a musical instrument. Playing a piano, violin, cello, trumpet, or banjo is not possible without the long and steady building of muscle memory. Itzhak Perlman, Yo-Yo Ma, and Wynton Marsalis are exceptional at what they do because they have developed unconscious and unlimited instructions for their body through decades of repeated practice. The longer you play an instrument, the faster your fingering and musical sight-reading become an extension of your mind and body. Our world's greatest musicians weren't born with the ability to play flawlessly. They were undoubtedly blessed with exceptional aptitude for developing their skills quickly, but they still had to start with the basics and grow from there. The repetitive motion of their fingers on the ivory of the piano or the strings of the instrument has become an extension of themselves. They no longer think about where an F# or C is; their fingers automatically respond to endless notations on sheet music. When you learn to type, you have to consciously think about where each letter is located on the QWERTY keyboard. After you become proficient, your muscle memory is so fast, it no longer requires conscious thought. You almost forget where the letters are. (With teenagers, it's different. After they become proficient at typing and texting, they forget where their parents are!)

A study in the *Journal of Applied Behavior Analysis* compared active and passive learning in preschoolers. The conclusions they reached were not surprising. One group of preschoolers was asked to copy basic ballet positions visually from their instructor, while the preschoolers in a second group had their bodies "placed" in each ballet position by their instructor. After a period, the preschoolers in the first group had developed faster and more accurate motor skill retention than the more passive preschoolers whose teachers had positioned their bodies. The first group developed faster because they were required to think and shape the positions on their own. The second group was allowed to be more passive and, therefore, less conscious of their direction. Careful, active study in the early stages of learning, as in group one, is extremely important for long-term skill development. Eventually, careful study leads to increased muscle memory retention. That is why it is important to learn a skill properly from the beginning. Once the skill is part of your muscle memory, it is difficult to un-learn it. (Which is why I'm always saying, "Once you know, you can't choose *not* to know anymore!") If something is learned wrong in the first place, it will often stay wrong. (I've learned this the hard way with downhill skiing. When I first learned, I looked like a foosball skier, and I still do!)

When you first learn basic tap dancing, throwing a baseball, or dribbling and shooting a basketball, it is difficult, and your form needs lots of conscious adjusting. However, after time and repetition, you are able to accomplish a time step or perform a layup without thought. The time step? I've totally got that down. The layup? Well . . . what's a layup again?

How is all this connected to autobiographical memory? Muscle memory is related to autobiographical memory because it is part of your life history. Remembering dance steps or how to ride a bicycle is part of your experience, part of what makes you the person that you are. The ability to recall your muscle memories of the past will allow you to excel in activities years after you first did them, like roller-skating or playing bridge when you get to the retirement home!

Besides the skills that live within us, our bodies seem to store the memories within the very fibers of our muscle tissue. Have you ever moved into a certain position, bumped yourself a particular way, or gotten a massage, and a memory came flooding back seemingly out of nowhere? Or what about assuming the posture of someone you know, and the memory of that person and their history with you fills your mind? (Or I don't know about you, but after a very sexy night, I have definitely been able to carry the memory of it in my body for days, and even years later!) Our bodies carry so much memory within them, in fact, that I've had several physical therapists relate stories of patients who have had major emotional breakthroughs while being massaged, manipulated, or rolfed! These are all examples of muscle memory in action, and they are directly connected to autobiographical memory!

A well-developed autobiographical memory, just like any other skill, can also be developed like muscle memory. The more you try to remember your past, the more it becomes second nature. The act of recording your life experiences evolves from the conscious to the habitual. Learning anything is a series of baby steps, including using your memory. Autobiographical memory development requires conscious, careful, deliberate effort at first, just as muscle memory does. When you approach development of your autobiographical memory in the same way that you develop muscle memory, the process is much faster and easier. It will also become second nature. Whenever you learn anything new, it seems like you're up against an impossible task. When looking back after you've reached a comfortable level of proficiency, it seems like the learning process was easy. It's all about perspective!

Music and Memory

Music is the answer for memories once forgotten.

—Unknown

No matter which of your senses is dominant, music is no doubt a powerful memory trigger. What mechanism can so readily bring tears to our eyes or joy to our heart? Whether it is the "Vissi d'arte" aria from Puccini's *Tosca,* Sting's "Fields of Gold" (my wedding song!), or something recent like Adele's "Someone Like You" (we all have that person!), music has the power to transport us back to a particular place and time. In an instant, we can relive a moment from our childhood, a beautiful romance, a painful breakup, a trip, a move, or just growing up. We can connect music to people, places, or things. Memories we had forgotten can flood back at the first bars of a song played on the radio, bringing with it the emotions we originally felt when we heard it. Music is boundless and all-encompassing, carrying our souls and allowing us to hold on to pieces of our lives without always realizing it. As Dick Clark once stated, "Music is the soundtrack of our lives."

Music is the binding thread that holds different peoples and cultures together. It is one of the few subjects that everyone connects and relates to, regardless of one's personal beliefs. One song can have several different memories and meanings for each separate individual who connects to it. For one person, it could represent a wild weekend they had, for another a divorce, and a third person may think back on their childhood dog who would do a silly dance every time he heard it. It doesn't matter if the tune is sad, happy, romantic, or rocking. A great aspect to the memory-music link is that it doesn't matter where the music comes from—memories can be created from any genre, even music we don't like.

Think back to certain movie soundtracks, TV show theme songs, or even world music you may have heard while traveling; you surely have images tied to each. Memories and their association with music aren't only connected to the Top 40 on the radio. Recollections attached to music are created without effort. You never know what song is going to affect you until it happens. This is why a couple's "song," for example, has so much weight behind it. You could be sitting in a restaurant with a date, already having listened to thirty different songs, but it is that *one* that suddenly changes the course of the evening. It isn't planned, but you unexpectedly connect to it. And, forevermore, when you hear that song, you think of that moment.

In the last few years, I've noticed that every girl under the age of fifteen has been scoring her life with the songs of Taylor Swift. No matter what kind of drama they have gotten themselves into in middle school, they make it more intense by going home and rocking out to "You Belong With Me" and "Mean." Why do they do that? Why do we love to listen to music when we are already in a particular mood? The answer is that there are times when we feel that the only person who could possibly understand us is not a person but a song, a piece of music. We listen to music to reinforce our emotions, which in turn reinforce our memories. If we are melancholy, we listen to somber music. If we are happy, we listen to spirited music. And if we are angry, we listen to aggressive music.

What I really love about music is that it is the closest thing human beings have to time-travel. As we get older, we change. This is a fact. We are not the same person we were at ten, sixteen, twenty, forty, or eighty! We are ever changing. Yet, when we hear a song that carries with it an emotion we once experienced, we can be ten or thirty years old again. For three minutes and twenty seconds, we can live in another time and place. We can see our parents, our friends from childhood, the places we've lived, wherever we've traveled, family gatherings, arguments we had, breakups, makeups, our first love—or our last. Music gives us the ability to reconnect with the person we once were in a way that nothing else can. The emotional memories we attach to music allow us the freedom to be another version of ourselves, a version that changes over time. I'm not saying we were better younger; far from it. But I think the power to reconnect with our youthful selves as mature adults has an interesting learning appeal. If at fifty years old we still behaved, felt, and thought as we did in our teens or twenties our daily lives would be chaos! The memories and emotions that music brings out in us are a chance to really see our growth.

Dr. Petr Janata, associate professor at the Center for Mind and Brain at the University of California–Davis, has been managing studies on memory and music. What he has discovered confirms what we already know: People have strong autobiographical memories associated with music. He has also found that people have vivid memories associated with not only the melody in a song, but also the title, the lyrics, and even the album cover or a photo of the artist.

EXERCISE: #9: MUSIC AND YOUR MEMORIES

When you hear a familiar song on the radio, what do you experience?

- Do you usually have memories connected to the title, the music, or the lyrics?
- How many of your senses can you engage when listening to music that has a powerful effect over you?
- What album cover instantly comes to mind when you read those two words?
- What type of music tends to bring back the most memories for you?

One of my favorite things to do while speed-walking is to listen to a whole album from a particular time in my life and relive the entire experience day by day. I can literally time-travel back to a whole vacation or work experience, or to every day in a relationship, or even revisit a full year if it's a very long walk! I recently listened to one of my all-time favorite albums, Sting's . . . *Nothing Like the Sun,* and recalled my top ten favorite days for every month of 1988! Why do I do this? Besides the fact that it's a blast to revisit places I've been and people I've seen, the greater lesson is in understanding the emotional life of that time, and one of the best ways for me to unlock that knowledge is through the music I'm listening to.

There is also a mentally therapeutic aspect to music. Since hearing is the last sense to leave us before we die, music has helped bring comfort to individuals in pain, as well as the loved ones emotionally suffering alongside them. Music is such a great comfort that music therapy is becoming increasingly practiced throughout the medical field due to its rehabilitative capacity. Musical therapists work with individuals of all ages (infants to seniors). They might work with people who have chronic pain, mental health concerns, substance abuse problems, or brain trauma, as well as those with developmental, learning, and physical disabilities, or even those looking for some relaxation and alleviation of mental stress. Therapists usually do not use a specific type of music since the healing potential depends on the individual's musical preference and what works best for their particular concerns. But in general soothing music has been proven to lower blood pressure, alter the heart rate, and relieve stress, so musical therapists tend to use it often in sessions.

In fact, music is so powerful as a memory tool that it has been known to help those with Alzheimer's and other degenerative brain diseases remember. According to a study conducted at the University of California–Irvine, Alzheimer's and dementia patients had better recall of objects, patterns, and shapes on memory tests while listening to classical music, specifically to Mozart. They found that music increases the release of certain hormones in the body that help to improve memory in both healthy and "unhealthy" people. Boston University has also released information on Alzheimer's and memory, unveiling that music not only helps patients remember old memories, but it also may help them form new ones. Alzheimer's patients were given several unfamiliar children's songs to listen to, half of which were spoken and half of which were sung. After a while they had to identify the songs again. The researchers compared the Alzheimer's patients' results to that of healthy adults of similar ages. According to the article published in *The Boston Globe,* "people with Alzheimer's correctly recognized 40 percent of the songs they heard sung compared with 28 percent of songs whose lyrics they heard spoken. The healthy adults didn't show as much of a difference." This is what allowed them to conclude that music may let Alzheimer's patients form new memories, although they are not positive what exactly about music (melody, rhyme, or rhythm) allows this to take place.

Music leaves an impression on everyone, whether young, old, healthy, or sick. Merriam-Webster's dictionary would have you believe that it is simply "the science or art of ordering tones or sounds in succession . . . to produce a composition having unity and continuity," but it is so much more. It embraces us in its folds when no one else can or will. Great melodies allow us to hold on to the things we once loved and over time forgot. They give us permission to be someone else, or to be the person we want to be. When we're weak they help us feel stronger, soothe away our pain and sorrow, and hold us close in moments of sad surrender. Music inspires, lifts us up to greater heights, and reminds us why life is worth the trouble. People will forever be connected to their memories as long as they are connected to music.

Chapter Four

The Charm Is in the Details

The true art of memory is the art of attention.

—*Samuel Johnson*

As an actress, I know that success is in the details. To effectively pull off a show one has to focus on everything that makes up the show—the writing, music, sets, costumes, hair, and makeup. I also believe there is much to be learned in doing things right and focusing on the small things to make a big success. I love to cook, to mother my children, to be there for my family. I cherish the details and remember each and every one. When I remember days long ago, I start out by locating myself on the number line of the year and then live in the memory as the details begin to float back to me, what we ate, the weather that day, where we stayed, whom we were with or about to see, my weight, how my hair looked, what seat I took in the car. These are the details to which I paid so much attention as a child, and I remember these details still.

One of my favorite plays of all time is *Our Town* by Thornton Wilder, and ever since I read it on Saturday, September 21, 1968, it resonated with my love for the beauty in the details. I saw parallels between the simple, family-oriented New England Protestants

Wilder depicts and my Polish Catholic family and neighbors. The play climaxes with Emily, a girl we've watched attend school, get married, and have kids, revisit her childhood now that she has died. She thinks going back to her twelfth birthday will satiate her hunger to be alive, that getting to relive it will be the same as living it the first time. She is fatally mistaken. Now that she has passed on, the details of her life take on more significance. She becomes incredibly upset seeing how quickly her family goes through their lives without taking the time to appreciate or notice their surroundings, their age, their emotions. The following dialogue takes place just after the memory ends:

> *Emily:* Do any human beings ever realize life while they live
> it? Every, every minute?
> *Stage Manager:* No. Saints and poets, maybe—they do
> some.
> *Emily:* I can't. I can't go on. It goes so fast. We don't have
> time to look at one another. (She breaks down sob-
> bing) . . . I didn't realize. So all that was going on
> and we never noticed. Take me back—up the hill—
> to my grave. But first: Wait! One more look. Good-by,
> Good-by, world. Good-by, Grover's Corners . . . Mama
> and Papa. Good-by to clocks ticking . . . and Mama's
> sunflowers. And food and coffee. And new-ironed
> dresses and hot baths . . . and sleeping and waking
> up. Oh, earth, you're too wonderful for anybody to
> realize you.

I love having the ability to remember every day of my life, be-cause I feel like I have an advantage in being able to see the whole picture, not just the extremes. It is not just the memories related to adrenaline that should be recalled, but also the simple, mundane,

Our Town slice-of-life memories. Most of us rarely remember many details from the daily routines we had as a child, or that of our parents, but these also hold meaning, often greater meaning than the memorable moments. These often tell the real story.

One of the reasons people don't remember much of their past is that they never received and processed the information the first time around. Students won't remember a lesson if they aren't focused during the lecture. For this very reason it is important to keep what I call your "attention units" on at all times. Sometimes we get so involved in and focused on our own thoughts, our feelings, our daily activities, and the way other people perceive us that our attention units shut down, and, as a result, we become unable to open ourselves up to new information and stimuli. This pattern of behavior blocks new memories and prevents restimulation of old memories. We can in turn become so insulated from the outside world that even simple data like the weather, time of day, day of the week, and so on cannot be taken in. How can we possibly expect to learn anything that's a little complex? All of these small factors color our experience and help plant it permanently in our memory. If some information is missing, it becomes difficult to link to the information that follows. That is why the goal of your Total Memory Makeover is to lead a more conscious life. Memory is a collection of information, so it becomes paramount that you don't limit that information by only receiving an abridged version of it. Try to keep those attention units open at all times. It is important to be conscious of everything surrounding you. Your antenna must constantly record information. Having a good memory requires awareness of where you are, what is around you, how you are feeling, and what is being said. The more information you receive, the more you are able to process and record.

There's a similar paradox in communication: The greatest speakers are also the greatest listeners. If you want to be a better speaker, lecturer, teacher, or just day-to-day conversationalist, then focus not on what you're going to say next, but rather on what the person you're talking to or the people you are lecturing to are saying and how they're reacting. They are your best guides to keeping yourself interesting, engaging, and on topic. Watch the late-night masters like David Letterman or Jay Leno. They are not concerned about saying their next joke because they know that the humor will come naturally as long as they stay connected to what the guest is saying and doing. They know that the best guide for responding is what the guest is saying, not what they "pre-thought" they should hear. That's what staying in the moment is all about. They carefully and continually observe everything that is going on: the guest, the audience, the set, the band, and everything else. And even better, they leave themselves open to anything that may change unexpectedly.

Being present is a skill worth developing for communication and practically everything else in life, especially memory. Our lives become so convoluted and we get so preoccupied with what we are going to do or say that we are unable to take in the necessary information that allows us to receive and remember. We become poor observers, because we are too busy watching ourselves.

The more information you receive, the more you are able to process and record. But that doesn't mean you should take in so much information at once that nothing can be absorbed, as is often the case with multitasking.

Multitasking has become a popular strategy for everyone these days, and, unfortunately, a bit of a necessity. The problem with multitasking is that because you're dividing your time between two or more activities, you're really only experiencing each at 50 percent (or less) capacity. If you're talking on the phone while watching your daughter's soccer game, you're only taking in half the game, not to mention half the conversation. You can't recall what you didn't fully experience. You have to dive in completely to create lasting memories. Try as often as you can to prioritize your tasks and focus 100 percent on one before moving on to the next. And be sure to focus on the information that's most important to you.

Anyone who has ever been in a relationship has had that conversation where you're certain you told your partner about important plans, but they are *just* as certain that you didn't. That's the result of listening with half an ear, because you're not engaged in any one thing. You might be able to walk and chew gum, but for tasks that require you to think, there needs to be a limit. You can't be half-available, so devote yourself to the task at hand. Then you can move on to the next and be totally present in *that* moment.

The "Juice"!

If you're going to embrace a life worth remembering, you need to find the "Juice"! The Juice is that element in the things we do that gets our blood pumping, our heart singing, and that memory-enhancing adrenaline rushing! We rarely forget the things we do when the Juice is flowing. Finding the Juice, therefore, offers a great strategy for remembering. It's also a great strategy for simply enjoying and getting the most out of your life.

When we are doing something we're passionate about, the Juice flows naturally. If you are passionate about travel, it's easy to find the Juice on a safari in Africa. If you're passionate about gardening, the Juice is blasting when you spot those first sprouting buds of spring. Granted, the Juice moments are wonderful, but we can't spend every waking hour engaged in the things that give us Juice. We have to do other things, too—go to work, do the laundry, feed the kids, clean the litter box, go to the dentist, and organize the garage. Where's the Juice in all of *that* stuff? Well, obviously, we don't have to enjoy or remember moments like that, right? Those are the moments we just try to get through as quickly as possible, so we can get back to the things we're passionate about, the things *with* the Juice. You can't enjoy everyday chores and obligations; it's as simple as that . . . right?

Well, I say, *"Wrong!* Why not?" Why shouldn't we enjoy the ordinary moments, as well? Why should we only take pleasure in one-third or even less of our time spent on this earth? The point I'm trying to make is that there could be Juice in *everything* we do; sometimes we just have to be a little more creative to find it. Take pride in washing and folding your laundry. Try making a game out of it. I know you're probably thinking, *All right, this time she's gone too far! Laundry? Who finds the Juice in doing their laundry?* Well believe it or not, my sister JoAnn finds doing her laundry one of the most meditative, therapeutic, and satisfying tasks ever. And on more than one occasion during our *Taxi* days, my good buddy Tony Danza would walk into the wardrobe room and say, "I'm feeling a little tense. Anybody got any ironing they want done?"

The Juice is where you find it!

Think how well your family reacts when you put a little love into your cooking, or about how happy your little kitty will be when he steps into the freshly cleaned litter box you took the time to prepare for him. Plan a stop on your way home from the dentist's office that could be exciting (a speed-walk through the park or the shopping mall), or you can simply take pride in your smooth, bright new smile after your teeth cleaning.

You have a choice: You can go to the dentist, do laundry, and clean the litter box. Or you can Go to the Dentist!!! Do Laundry!!! And Clean the Litter Box!!! Attitude is everything and the bottom line is that it's difficult to remember the days in your life, or the life in your days, that were Juice-less. My mantra is "Juice-less days are useless days" . . . at least when it comes to relishing and remembering them. If a person with average memory can accurately recall only about ten events from the previous year, and a person with Highly Superior Autobiographical Memory can accurately recall two hundred or more, perhaps those of us in the latter group are simply finding a little Juice in everything we do.

But maybe it's not about an adrenaline-pumping experience for you. Maybe a sense of peace and relaxation sounds juicier. That's great! Believe it or not, one of my daily tasks that I consider at the top of my Juice chart is driving my kids to school. Many parents complain about the grind and commitment it takes, but I absolutely cherish that time with them. It is one of those moments I am still able have with them before they both start driving on their own and are too embarrassed to be seen with Mom. It might only be for half an hour each way, but it is worth its weight in gold to me. Try to find those little pockets of *Our Town*–type memories that are enjoyable for you. Try to find that little piece of gold, that spoonful of sugar, in everything you do each day. Once you become aware of what makes a moment special, those kinds of experiences will become more frequent.

As an experiment, I explained the concept of Juice to several friends and family members and asked them what was the first thing that came to mind after I'd explained the whole idea. Kaisha, my brother Lorin's wife, immediately said that the best example of Juice is her first date with Lorin. This is obviously a memory she knows well and loves to recall. She can instantly remember and re-create the shyness she felt, the way my brother's clothes smelled like clean linen, and how *small* she felt beside him. She mentioned that if she went through that date moment to moment, she could bring that day back, as if it had just happened. All the feelings she experienced that night rush back and give her a natural, positive high. Finding the Juice is easiest when you start with something with which you have a strong connection.

We all have these kinds of memories, these happy moments upon which we love to dwell, and you will find, as you go through this process, that these incidents pop up more often as you stimulate your memory. For instance, hearing Kaisha's enthusiasm triggered a whole montage of important romantic dates for me. I can literally relive every great date I've had in my life. If you get into that mind-set, you can do it with practically every experience.

My First Date with Michael

When I look back on my first date with Michael, it helps me better understand him in the present. A little back story first: He and I had met our freshman year at the University of Chicago (Friday, October 9, 1970) but never dated, as he was my roommate's boyfriend. Years later (on Friday, September 26, 1980) we had run into each other in a courthouse in New Orleans when I was getting a marriage license with my first (soon to be ex) husband. Twenty-two and a half years passed with absolutely no contact, but he had called to reconnect with me on Saturday, February 22, 2003, and now we were having what I hoped would turn into a real date on Saturday, March 1, 2003. I could go into every minute detail about that evening, but what was so telling was that Michael wore an outfit that night that was completely different from the way he dresses now. He actually wore a billowy cream-colored shirt with front-pleated MC Hammer pants (thirteen years after "U Can't Touch This") and looked like a Brazilian R and B hipster . . . from Utah. Nothing matched. It made his stomach look big and sucked the color out of his skin tone; believe it or not, he looked like he was trying too hard. I know now that before our date he asked his daughters, both in their early twenties at the time, to help him. On our second date, after he was a lot more comfortable; he wore a black T-shirt and jeans and a jacket. And I thought, This looks right! This fits his persona much more. Michael has a very big, strong presence. He is much bigger and much more powerful looking than I am, so it's easy to overlook his softer side. I often flash back to that day just to remind myself of his vulnerability and how important our first date was to him. Looking back helps me see the whole picture of who he really is and not just what is happening in the present. I love that outfit now because of its significance. Even though it was horrible for him style- and color-wise, I saved it in our closet, just because it's from our first date.

Keeping that kind of personal information fresh heightens one's sensitivity to other people and helps you read the clues they send out. You definitely become less critical and more appreciative because you see all the subtleties in a person's character and not just extremes. This is not to say that you should be overly accepting of the creeps out there, no matter how many nice things they try to do to balance out their bad behavior. An extensive memory resource allows you to see things the way they really are, as well as know which people to avoid.

Opening up your receptors now will not only allow you to re-create great past experiences; you will also develop new ones with greater detail. When you go through a first date or something equally exciting, you are in a heightened state of awareness, and as a result you will relive it in your mind several times—whether it was good or bad! You will be able to turn a lot of average days into something more special, because you will go into every experience with a more sharpened level of awareness, which will undoubtedly lead to better recall. Instead of being someone who just plods along living a life of quiet desperation, crank up the volume and turn on the *Juice*!

EXERCISE #10: ADDING THE JUICE

Spend the rest of this day consciously thinking about squeezing a little more Juice into everything you're doing.

- As you do this, think about how much this affects your memory of each moment. In fact, check back tomorrow to see how much you can remember from the time you were engaged in this exercise.
- Also, think about the things in your life that automatically have the Juice, those activities that fire you up without any effort.
- The next time you engage in one of those activities, pay attention to how your receptors are working compared to other, less passionate activities. Once you know this information, you will be able to see where you're Juicy and where you're drying up.

Your Memory Landscape

No memory is ever alone; it's at the end of a trail of memories, a dozen trails that each have their own associations.

—*Louis L'Amour*

Normally, we like to think that things develop in a linear, step-by-step manner. We look at our lives in much the same way as we would the narrative of a story; one thing follows another, and then another, in an orderly style. You wouldn't tell the middle of a story and then the end and then jump back to the beginning. (Unless you're Harold Pinter, of course!) In the same way, when we work on problems, chores, and projects, we naturally try to complete them in this organized chronological direction. Memory retrieval and memory construction, however, are different.

For example, as a memory is retrieved, does it always surface in your mind the same way? Not for me. Sometimes, if given a date, I see the events of the date in chronological order. Sometimes, I'll recall my day from the moment I woke up and see it all unfold in an orderly fashion. But just as often, I can spark the events of the day or any type of memory by coming at it from different directions. The mechanics of memory retrieval are unpredictable. Memories are reconstructed, changed, and enlarged each time they're retrieved. They're malleable but get stronger with each recall.

Your memory is extremely complicated, with millions of intricate, weblike patterns and connections of synapses located throughout your vast brain network. It's not just one system, but a group of systems playing different roles, which creates, stores, processes, and recalls information. These interconnected systems work together to produce thoughts and retrieve memories. Memory and memory retrieval are so complicated, and the process to access and organize memories is also complicated. Retrieval not only comes in many forms, it often comes without our consent or control, like dreaming. Thankfully, we have more control when we're awake, but—don't kid yourself—not total control!

I categorize memory retrieval into four groups: Horizontal, Vertical, Mushrooming, and Sporadic. Let's look at each of these separately. In order to demonstrate the differences among the four types of memory retrieval, let's use as an example a weekend wedding you might have attended in the past.

Horizontal memory is the easiest to understand because it is linear, chronological, and relatively simple to follow. We use Horizontal memory to try to organize our thoughts when we recount an event as a whole. This kind of retrieval tends to stay on the surface of our minds rather than deep in our thoughts, as it avoids too much detail. It's the way we would recount our daily schedule when describing to someone how we spent our day.

Thinking of our sample wedding weekend: Starting with that initial Friday evening event, you would probably think back and start at the beginning of the whole weekend by recounting the rehearsal for the wedding ceremony, followed by the rehearsal dinner for the wedding party and out-of-town guests. After that, you might conjure up the image of a group of you gathering in the lobby of the hotel before saying good night. Then you would picture the next morning, getting ready for the big event, followed by the wedding ceremony itself and the cocktail hour, and concluding with dinner and dancing. Before moving on to the next moment, you briefly see in your mind each of these activities. For the most part, this is done chronologically, without getting stuck on any one activity for too long. Horizontal memory retrieval moves along in a relatively quick, horizontal, linear direction.

Vertical memory goes much deeper than Horizontal memory and is more detailed with any selected experience. Rather than moving from one activity to the next, while barely touching down, you go deeper and deeper into each particular moment. Using the same wedding weekend as an example, you flash back to a moment at the reception and remember feeling particularly nostalgic. *What happened again?* you think to yourself. *Oh, right!* And suddenly you remember waiting for the reception line and running into your cousin Lisa, whom you hadn't seen for many years. You laugh to yourself as you remember your conversation about how neither of you had changed, when in reality you were thinking how the passage of time hadn't been kind to her and wondering if she were thinking the same about you. You keep going deeper and deeper into the memory of standing there talking to Lisa, and you're remembering Lisa's face and what she wore and what you wore and how the room looked, and you can suddenly see the pattern of the wallpaper behind her, and hear what music was playing at the time, and remember how the history of the two of you came flooding back as you both stood there and continued to talk about the family and what everyone was doing now. The more you talked, the more relaxed and close you felt. So close, in fact, that her entire physiognomy changed, and you both once again looked like the best-friend teenage cousins you used to be.

If you really tried, you could probably do this for the entire evening, going deeper and deeper and more specifically into the details of that one weekend event. But it's not just about the *who* or *what;* it's more about the *why* and the subtext. I call it Vertical memory retrieval, because it explores the deeper feelings associated with each event. The more you think about an event, the deeper you can delve into each memory, re-creating each moment with more and more psychological detail.

Mushrooming memory is where memory can get a bit out of control. In this type of memory retrieval, memories grow from one particular source. Using the wedding example again, these Mushroom memories would be the ones that stem from that night or that three-day event. They are the relatives, friends, visits, opportunities, or events you later experienced because of whatever happened during the wedding weekend itself. You made a business connection that turned into a job opportunity that then created new memories. You sat next to the groom's former roommate, who invited you to visit his hometown, and consequently the time spent there with him and his friends becomes a memory that stems from the original wedding event. New events and memories have "Mushroomed" out from that other, original experience.

Sporadic memory retrieval is similar to Mushrooming, because it is triggered by its similarity to a particular experience, but it is not actually connected to the original source the same way Mushroom memory is. These are memories sparked in your mind for no apparent reason, random images that pop into your head seemingly disconnected from what is going on in present time. They are Sporadic thoughts, triggered by associations in your head that only you can dig deep enough to identify.

Going back to the wedding again, for example, you remember the DJ playing a song that reminded you of a special moment in high school. Suddenly, you've time-traveled back to that memory, which has nothing to do with this wedding, other than that song. You recall spotting someone in the wedding party who looks like your old boss, and *voilà!* You're back on that job behind your desk dealing with his personality. The memory of the taste of the wedding cake frosting instantly takes you back to that French patisserie on the Left Bank with its special dessert. Sporadic recall is much more random and usually beyond our control. It just happens automatically. It is Sporadic because of the similarity to how spores journey and plant themselves randomly in nature. We can become more aware of Sporadic recall, but, for the most part, it's arbitrary and capricious. We can't always predict it. Memories can seem spontaneous or Sporadic when they are stimulated by just anything, even if it is our own random thoughts.

It may seem unimportant to trace memories in this way, but it becomes a very powerful memory tool. Connecting your experiences and memories makes them much easier to locate and retrieve. This helps keep them alive. Without making this conscious effort, those memories eventually exist as isolated little islands, unlabeled moments anchored to practically nothing. And more often than not, they can fade in your mind to a point where you can no longer remember them.

The main point to take away from all of this is that memory works in many different modes and directions. There is no right or wrong way to remember. Controlling memory stimulation and where it takes you can be almost as difficult as controlling a dream, and you have to accept that. Any incident in your life has the potential to be recalled in any of these patterns. Whether it's Horizontally, Vertically, Mushroomingly (yes, that is a word!), or Sporadically, there's no wrong way for memories to form. These patterns of mental association help anchor weaker memories to stronger memories, which keeps both types from fading. And the more familiar you are with these patterns, the easier it will be for you to travel from one to the next.

EXERCISE #11: MEMORY PRIMERS

I will give you one of the exercises the memory team at UC Irvine gave me the very first time I was tested:

Think back to your twenty-first birthday.

- What is the first memory that comes up when you read the question?
- What do you remember about that day?
- What did you do?
- What images come to mind?

- Are you remembering your twenty-first birthday in a chronological order? Or are you thinking about one part of the day and staying fixated on that part, as you delve deeper and deeper in the memory?
- Maybe you're remembering a particular person from that night and what you did with them on another occasion. Or perhaps there is an image or a song or smell you can remember from that night that transports you to another day and time, or even another birthday.

Start becoming aware of how you recall things when you start with one event or one memory.

Now try to remember the same birthday in the four different ways we've discussed throughout this chapter: Horizontally, Vertically, Mushroomingly, and Sporadically.

Each original memory or event will probably be remembered in a different way. Unlock your brain and unleash your memories. Feel free to be more open to whatever comes up. Your brain is the result of all the circuitry and wiring, and by understanding the route your memories prefer to take, the way your brain retrieves things, you can set it up and utilize it to its full potential. For example, if you tend to prefer to recall a memory in a linear way, the next time you try to remember something, walk yourself through the memory using the Horizontal method. Let's say you're trying to remember a Saturday evening with friends; you may have to start even earlier in the day or even the day before to remember the specifics of that evening. In other words, when remembering, play to your memory strengths.

Unlocking Your Memory Blocks

⹂he repressed memory is like a noisy intruder being thrown out of the concert hall. You can throw him out, but he will bang on the door and continue to disturb the concert. The analyst opens the door and says, "If you promise to behave yourself, you can come back in."

—Theodor Reik

One morning, as a preparation exercise for a memory class I was teaching, I asked my husband, Michael, to go over past vacations we've shared. I wanted to see how many details we could recall together. For me, of course, this was fun. I enjoy the game of putting the puzzle pieces together and watching the images emerge. I can immediately see each event as it connects to other events; one memory triggers another, and then another, and so on. For Michael, however, this exercise wasn't as enjoyable. As we went over our 2004 trip to Venice, for example, I was describing every restaurant at which we ate, the routes we took while speed-walking in the morning, what we both wore each day, and the little shops where we stopped. Some of these descriptions triggered memories for Michael, and he, too, remembered additional activities and moments, but eventually, he reached a point where he just couldn't remember any more details. He claimed that he hit a "block" and could go no further. He said he wanted to remember but couldn't.

He may have really hit some kind of block, or perhaps he was just bored or overwhelmed by the exercise. I may have been driving him crazy with too much information! (After all, not many guys care about the cafés and glass shops they passed while speed-walking on a vacation seven years ago!) But I was intrigued by the differences

Michael and I experienced in our desire and ability to recall our trips. It was more than my having HSAM. Michael is the number one trivia expert in our family, so I know he has an unbelievable memory for many things. But in this case, did he just not care to go further? Was he having an off day, or is there really something that holds him back from remembering? Is it fear? Is it that he is like some people who consciously block their past? What could they (and possibly Michael) be avoiding? Is there an immovable block, or do they just need a little push? I would love Michael to enjoy developing his autobiographical memory as much as I do.

Next, I asked my brother Lorin and his wife, Kaisha, to try the same "past vacations" exercise together. I wondered if either would have the same blocks and resistance as Michael. They eventually came back with entirely different answers. Kaisha said she didn't exactly run into a block; it was more like the information was there, but it was vague. She felt that she could remember most of the things that happened, but the details were a little fuzzy and diluted. Lorin felt that much of his memory had gaps or holes. Some pieces were missing completely. He jokingly claimed that he suffered from SCS—"Swiss Cheese Syndrome."

Lorin feels he has a tendency to "lock in" too much on certain moments, but then he excludes other points that follow. He has trouble remembering some things when trying to recall them later, because it's difficult to remember what you didn't hear in the first place. He explained, for example, that when he is listening to someone, in a conversation or at a lecture, he's often transfixed by one point that is brought up. He then goes deeper and deeper in his mind, analyzing that point, comparing it to other thoughts and past experiences. Meanwhile, the person he's conversing with, or the lecturer he's listening to, has moved on to other points, which Lorin is now missing. I know that may sound strange and confusing, but this is fairly common. It is called overanalyzing disorder. It is also known as overthinking disorder. This comes, he feels, from his tendency to overthink in general.

Lorin, however, is grateful he has this condition. He embraces it because although he misses many surface moments, he benefits by frequently diving deep into his "selected" thoughts, which helps him reach insights he would not have discovered if he were always hanging out "on the surface." He remembers some things in great detail, even though his memory has got a lot of holes in it, hence "Swiss Cheese Syndrome." But Lorin quickly adds, "On the plus side, my memory goes delightfully well with a glass of Pinot Noir!" If Lorin has Swiss cheese memory, then Kaisha may have . . . skim milk memory? Either way, it's pretty clear that these two are suffering from too much dairy!

The real conclusion here is that people have varying needs, abilities, and objectives in remembering their pasts, and there are dozens of reasons people stumble in their efforts to do so. I believe, from what I've observed in my memory classes, that anyone who is willing to examine what is causing his or her memory block can get past it *if* the desire to remember is strong enough. You have to be ready to try different solutions, beginning with examining what you want to accomplish and what obstacles (if any) could be stopping or slowing you down. You have to ask yourself why you can't or don't want to remember. For Michael and Kaisha, and the majority of my memory class students, they might just need "triggers" (i.e., pictures, video, documents, or discussing the event with other people), and Lorin (along with the other "cheese heads") needs to stay on topic more or just accept the fact that some things will be missed.

Everyone is unique, and everyone needs to come to the memory table ready to play if they're to make any real headway. But people do differ in their willingness and desire to remember the past. Some would go to great lengths to remember, and others really don't care at all; then there are those who don't even want to think about it. Most people are somewhere in between.

It's like Facebook. Some people want nothing to do with it, while others are obsessively on there all the time. About half a billion people, however, enjoy it simply for what it is—a great new entertainment and pastime. In a similar way, developing your memory, especially your autobiographical memory, can become a great, new, rewarding, and enlightening hobby. A life worth living is a life worth remembering. When it comes to memory, where do you fit in? How much do *you* want to remember? Are you ready to "play"?

EXERCISE #12: MEMORY BLOCKS

Take a moment and try to remember an event from ten years ago. Once you have selected an event, jot down a list of everything you can remember. Don't write a narrative of what happened, just a word or phrase that labels each item you remember. I gave this exercise to my number one test subject, Lorin, and this is what he came up with for a wedding he attended in Wisconsin in March of 2003 (I guess he wanted to stay with a cheese-head theme):

1. The hotel room (crowded and noisy)
2. The layout of the church and reception hall
3. The location of the open bar at the reception hall (his most vivid memory of all)
4. The dollar dance with the bride
5. Dancing with the bride's mother and grandmother

After you've made a brief list of what you remember, incorporate other resources (such as photos) to get past memory blocks and build on your list. Lorin thought he had nothing left, but here's what he came up with after looking at just two photos from the event:

1. Walking around the neighborhood of the church
2. How beautiful the bride and bride's mother looked that day
3. How tightly packed the tables were at the reception
4. Specific conversations at dinner
5. The bride's aunt challenging other women (and men) to arm-wrestle
6. The funny toast made by the best man
7. Some of the people from another wedding held next door
8. The party favors on each table
9. The bride and groom describing their honeymoon plans

What I'm hoping you'll discover from this exercise is that just a few triggers (for Lorin it was just two photographs) can bring back many other memories from an event as far as ten years away. Don't ever stop when you think you've reached a block; think of links that can get you deeper into the memory.

Missing Memory Story

A Highly Superior Autobiographical Memory can sometimes have a downside . . . for others! I'm sure my memory is sometimes annoying for the rest of my family because I remember many things that my siblings don't. I've gotten better about not torturing them with this, I'm sure I've driven them crazy over the years. It's a great way to win arguments . . . but lose friends! Sometimes, though, I just can't help myself. Recently I was reminiscing about an event with my sister JoAnn, who recounts the following:

A few months ago, Marilu began our morning phone call by talking about Nicky, who had recently gotten his driver's license and, LA traffic being what it is, she was worried about potentially scary driving situations. I think immediately we both thought back to a time when she was about twelve and I was twenty-one.

She said to me, "Remember that time we were driving on the Kennedy Expressway where it meets the Edens and the tire just came off the car? You expertly maneuvered the car onto that small piece of land, right between the two expressways. Remember? Can you remember that was almost fifty years ago, on Sunday, April 12, 1964? You were about five months pregnant with Lizzy, and we were on our way to Notre Dame Boys High School because you were choreographing Wonderful Town *there."*

I remembered the incident all too well. In fact, to this day, I think about it every time I am driving up the Kennedy. We were in my aqua 1953 Ford and I grabbed that steering wheel with more force than I knew I had.

But I answered, "It wasn't Wonderful Town. *I was choreographing* South Pacific."

"No," she said, "It was Wonderful Town."

I said, "Marilu, it can't have been Wonderful Town. *I never did* Wonderful Town, *I don't really even know the show."*

She said, "Are you kidding me? You choreographed the number "Wrong Note Rag" that very day. I could still show you. I can still do the choreography for that number."

We went on discussing it for quite a while, and I was getting upset about it because I know that she is almost always right, but even with her prodding I couldn't remember having done Wonderful Town. *I was so sure I was right; I was convinced she was wrong.*

I should have probably let it go, but I couldn't. Besides, I needed to prove to myself that I hadn't misrepresented a memory that was so vivid and exact. (Big sisters can make you lose your confidence!) The next day, I called Notre Dame High School and said, "Hi, this is Marilu Henner. I got my start in show business when I was in fifth grade and in your school's production of *South Pacific* in 1963. My older sister JoAnn choreographed that show and another show the following year in 1964 called *Wonderful Town*. Do you guys by any chance have any programs or anything at all in your archives from those shows? I would be so grateful if you could find anything from that time that shows if either of us was involved in those productions." Two days later, scans of photos and programs from the two productions arrived in my in-box! I couldn't believe it. I was ecstatic! It was a blast going over all the names and reminiscing about all of the great people in those shows, but more important was the moment when I saw JoAnn's name listed as . . . choreographer! Just as I remembered, of course. It was the proof I needed to win an argument with my big sister and well worth the wait! *Wonderful Town?* You bet!

Partners in Memory

Memories naturally trigger other memories. This is an important point that will come up often in your memory journey. Even though Michael did have trouble remembering our 2004 Venice trip, he was eventually able to remember more just by trading memories back and forth with me. Lorin and Kaisha did a similar exercise and eventually got similar results. They provided lots of triggers and connections for each other, just as Michael and I did. Nothing helps open the floodgates more effectively than exchanging memories with someone who shared the experience with you.

You may not be able to bring back every moment, but just having a partner makes it easier and a lot more fun to fill in the blanks together. Imagine then what could be accomplished when you bring three or four people into this memory mix, which is what Lorin, Kaisha, and I tried with a shared family trip, the Henner Family Christmas in New York, 2007. At first, they could only remember a few highlights, but eventually every day, each meal, and all the events came flooding back. Believe it or not, almost every one of the sights, smells, tastes, emotions, and memories was brought to the surface by a few prompting questions from me to get them started. Lorin and Kaisha were thrilled, because they hadn't thought about these moments for almost four years, and we practically reenacted our entire trip!

It's important to do this every once in a while with the memories you want to keep alive. Reliving those holiday weeks in New York gave us an extended warranty, so to speak, on that event in our lives. Without doing this for important memories, it's very easy for them to fade to a point where only a séance will bring them back.

Occasional recollection is essential for keeping memories present. When I go back and think about a particular place, like Venice, I don't just think about my last visit there. I automatically see each of the four trips I've taken there, from my first visit in 1976 to shoot a Wisk "Ring around the collar" commercial, to two trips with my second husband, Rob, in January 1986 and September 1988, and the one with Michael and my sons in 2004. When I think about each trip, every memory comes flooding back. I remember my daily morning jog route, the little bakery I always passed or stopped at to get a torte. I can still see the faces of the people who worked there. As I'm thinking about this, I can even hear the songs that were playing on the radio during one of my visits. I love doing this exercise, and it is very rewarding for me. It's like world-traveling and time-traveling rolled into one. One of the biggest reasons this is easy for me is because I do it often. As much fun as this is on my own, it's even more fun to do it with others.

Make it a point to try this memory assignment with someone while you are reading this book. You will both exercise your memory and stimulate your emotional connections to those memories. Later in the book, we'll do these exercises with the help of photographs, videos, and diaries, but I feel it is important to begin this exercise on your own without help from other visual or audio aids.

EXERCISE #13:

Do the same memory-blocks exercise that you did in Exercise #12, but this time, pick another event from ten or even fifteen years ago. Write out a list of what you remember first, without any help. When you reach a block, instead of looking at a photo or other object to spark memories, contact someone else who experienced that event with you. Have a memory brainstorming session to try to bring back as many memories from it as possible. Hopefully, you'll find a great deal more than you did using an object as a memory trigger, as you did in the last exercise. This exercise not only can be fun, it can also be informative for your relationship with that person and the progress in your own life.

Marilu and I first met as fellow actor/performers in community theater in Chicago over forty-three years ago. From almost the very beginning, we have always engaged in a very strange ritual or game of Test Your Memory whenever we see each other, talk on the phone, or send one another the occasional card or letter.

The Test Your Memory game will usually begin with a name, one from the distant past—the more obscure the better. Perhaps it's a third replacement chorus boy understudy from a production of The Boy Friend *back in 1968. I might call her and when she picks up I'll say, "Uh, yes, is Hamish Menzies there, please?" Howls of laughter go up, followed by, "Jacobs, you nut! Uh, well no, Hamish is off today, but Valerie Van Wolf is here." More laughs. This silly back-and-forth banter may go on for several minutes before I finally give in and say, "Who?"*

—Jim Jacobs

Up till now, you've learned the "who, what, when, where, why, and how" of your autobiographical memory. It's time to start using it. In the next chapter, we will find your Track and start building the timeline of your life!

Part Two

PARTICIPATION

Your Unforgettable Life

Chapter Five

The Track That Takes You Back

Memory is funny. Once you hit a vein the problem is not how to remember but how to control the flow.

—*Tobias Wolff*

Find Your Track

Remembering and documenting your life can range from being really simple to being quite extensive and complex. It depends on how much you want to get involved and how much time you want to invest. The more effort and detail you put into it, the greater the rewards. It's your choice. The beauty of this project is that even a little effort will bring great rewards. It can also go on for the rest of your life. Like genealogy research and constructing your roots and family tree, you don't have to commit much at first. You can do a lot in the beginning or just a little to get your feet wet, and then change your pace and commitment later. Some days, you might be inspired to work on it a lot, and other days, you'll make just a brief effort or none at all. Eventually, though, you're going to have constructed a timeline of your life. It will become the ultimate reference for remembering, analyzing, and getting an overview of your entire history, which is a valuable resource very few people ever have.

You need a good place to start, and the first step is finding your Track! Actually, we all have many tracks, but I'm talking about your main Track. Finding one Track will help you find other tracks, and before you know it, you will have a whole rail system of tracks and be well on your way to reconstructing the story of your life.

What exactly do I mean by your "Track"? In discussing memory for so many years, I have come to realize that we all have primary connections, or tracks, for remembering things. Magnetized by your truest passions, your main Track is probably where your mind goes when you should be working or doing your everyday chores. For example, some guys can't remember what they ate for dinner last night but can tell you exact stats, precise scores, specific dates, and detailed double plays from a baseball game they watched when they were a kid. They can even tell you what they were drinking, who was pitching, how many points were scored, who was the hero, and why they lost by one point in a game played thirty-five years ago.

Many guys have a sports track, but a Track could be anything: career, relationships, travel, children, outfits, meals, exercise habits, living spaces, money issues, business ventures, and so on. The author/director Nora Ephron wrote about women and their remembering clothes and men in the play *Love, Loss, and What I Wore*, which sounds very similar to one of my many tracks, "Boys and My Weight"! (You may be thinking that Nora and I have *two* main tracks, but because each one is so connected to the other, we both apparently consider them part of the same track!) We'll start building your greater autobiographical memory by identifying your main Track, because everyone remembers something exceptionally well and in great detail. It really depends on the person and what is most important or has the greatest impact emotionally. Believe me, I've even heard *bats*!

While working on the Discovery Channel's *Curiosity* series episode about memory, the host Dan Riskin told me his Track was bats, and he wasn't kidding! So there we were (on Tuesday, June 22, 2010), at Bracken Cave in San Antonio with four million bats flying over our heads at dusk. Just from Dan's being near those bats and telling me stories about his love for them, his memories about so many other things came flooding back. After that experience, I was more convinced than ever—everyone has a Track!

Think of your life and all your past experiences as an enormous five-thousand-piece jigsaw puzzle scattered about your house. You haven't lost the pieces. They are all still there, but they need to be located and reconnected, so you can see the whole picture. Other than raising a child, I can't think of a more exciting project! The reason it's inspiring to begin with your Track is because those will be the easiest jigsaw pieces to find. Your Track pieces are like the straight-edged border pieces of the puzzle. Their well-defined shape stands out and easily catches your eye, even when you can't identify the image on the piece. There are fewer of them, so they're relatively quick to link together into a pattern. After you've built the border on a jigsaw puzzle, you move inward, connecting middle pieces to those that are already in place. You can't randomly place pieces in the middle; you need other properly placed pieces to link with them. Connecting the puzzle pieces of your life works the same way. You start with the pieces that are easiest to identify and place, your Track pieces, which then provide a pattern for finding the more obscure pieces, which are usually difficult to find without having a connection first.

Eventually, you will be placing these dates in your timeline, which is the grand framework of your autobiographical memory. It will be the schematic of your life. But first, your Track will provide the initial pieces of that timeline. (Or, as my brother-in-law, renowned architect William Drake, understands it, "In the murky forest of your memory, what pebbles have you dropped along the way?")

Finding your Track is easy. You probably identified your Track as soon as I defined what a memory Track is. If you're still unsure, it may be because, like most people, you have more than one main Track. It doesn't matter. Your Track is mainly a tool and guide to get you started on your timeline. Pick any category that is important to you, something that you think will be a good foundation to help you remember your past. The point is to discover and analyze how you elicit memories, using something you're passionate about. After that, you can apply that same process to everything else in your life to help reconstruct your past.

IDENTIFYING YOUR TRACK

In case you are having trouble identifying your Track, here are a few questions to help you. After completing the questionnaire, analyze your answers. Your Track should be obvious.

Track Questionnaire

1. When you walk into a bookstore or library, what is the first section you usually visit?

2. When you first meet new people, what topic do you tend to discuss with them?

3. When people come to you for advice it is usually on what subject?

4. What are the five best gifts you've ever received for special occasions in your life?

5. What are the five best gifts you've *given* for special occasions to other people?

6. What were your five most memorable birthdays and why?

7. What were the five best days of your life and why?

8. What are the five most popular words people use to describe you?

9. Describe in detail your ideal party.

10. Describe in detail your ideal date.

Rate the following activities on a one-to-ten scale based on your passion for each. Ten equals strongest feelings and one means you couldn't care less.

1. Reading
2. Watching TV
3. Family time
4. Going to the movies
5. Exercise
6. Listening to music
7. Entertaining
8. Playing sports
9. Shopping
10. Traveling
11. Sleeping

12. Socializing
13. Church activities
14. Housework
15. Crafts
16. Attending sports
17. Playing cards
18. Hiking
19. Cooking
20. Dining out
21. Working on cars
22. Animal care
23. Volunteer work
24. Dancing
25. Pampering

Have any categories jumped out at you? If you're still having trouble, ask someone close to you to analyze your answers. Sometimes we're too close to the action to see the big picture.

Your tracks are easiest to trace back. If, for example, your first love is travel, you probably could recall every trip you've taken in the last thirty years, including the year, usually the right month, and maybe even the exact day. You may even remember most of the activities you did on those trips, as well. Remember APR? It's naturally built into travel. We look forward to it with eager anticipation, by counting down the days on a calendar. We often plan what we are going to do each day, to get the most out of our travel time, and that also helps lock certain dates into our memory. We make every day count, which is the participation phase at full throttle. Finally, we almost always take photographs and videos of our trips; both of these document the experience, which we relive every time we view them. This is the ultimate in recollection. No wonder travel is a popular Track!

On the other hand, perhaps your Track is your career. People with a career track can usually relate every birthday, anniversary, and holiday to what job they had and even what project they were in the middle of at the time. Because one of my many tracks is "Boys and My Weight," I can tell you detailed information about every guy I've ever dated, along with how much I weighed on each date, sometimes as specific as before and *after* dinner! My sister Christal is a world-class contract bridge champion and also a connoisseur of fine restaurants. Those are her two main tracks. In the last twenty-eight years, she can tell you not only how she placed in every major and regional tournament and in what city each tournament was held; she can also tell you every great meal she had throughout each tournament!

Use Your Track to Take You Back

School is one track we all have in common. Even if it was never your passion, everyone has a school track. Because school is a common denominator for all of us, many of the exercises I use in my memory classes today stem from the school-related questions that I used to ask myself when I was growing up. Each school year, I would think, *Okay, what was I doing this week last year? What was I doing the first day of freshman year? Sophomore? What did I do the first week of school when this happened or that happened? What did I do on this day five years ago, or ten years ago?* School was a natural track to use, because school is organized by years and semesters, which already does much of the structuring for us.

At a lecture I gave recently for three hundred people, I asked, "By a show of hands, how many of you think you can reconstruct your entire schedule from freshman year of high school?" No one raised a hand. Then I asked, "Okay, now think this through carefully and try to reconstruct it class by class, writing it out in your notebooks. Think about your first class, perhaps your last class, the class before lunch, where you walked, what time each bell rang, what you were studying, who some of the teachers were, what the classrooms looked like, tests you took that year, your best friends, kids that mistreated you, the brainiacs, the flakes, the grades you got, anything at all that could connect and trigger memories. Eventually, it should come to you piece by piece in building blocks. When you're confident that you've completed your entire schedule, look up from your notebook and raise your hand for a few seconds, so I can get a sense of how long this takes everyone. Don't be influenced by peer pressure to finish early. I might even give a prize to the last person to finish."

Moments after I explained this assignment, I saw one hand go up in front. It was a girl about fifteen years old. In a teasing way I said, "That's cheating! You probably just finished your freshman year." But I then watched hands go up one by one throughout the auditorium. After five minutes, I stopped them, because nearly half the audience had finished. I could tell that most of the people were pleased and surprised that they could put all the pieces together after so many years.

This exercise is a great example of how memory is all about connections. One memory leads to the next in a pattern that makes sense to your brain. No matter how your memories are accessed (Horizontally, Vertically, Mushroomingly, or Sporadically) you reach them through the process of association.

To see the process up close, I asked my brother Lorin to try writing out his entire class schedule for all four years in high school, starting with his freshman year. His first thought was that the task would be impossible. He said, "Sure, I can give it a shot, but there's no way it will be accurate!" He was skeptical but willing to try. Right away, he was certain that woodshop was his first class starting at eight A.M., because he remembered being reprimanded by his woodshop teacher for being tardy several times. He was also certain that his last class that year was biology, because the teacher was very strict and he remembered many occasions of eagerly waiting for the clock to reach the 2:32 P.M. bell. After realizing that specific times on the clock (daily markers along the school track) helped spark some memories, he wrote up the daily schedule by class period. He knew the first class started at eight A.M. and each class was forty minutes long with a four-minute break between each period:

1st period 8:00 A.M.–8:40 A.M.
2nd period 8:44 A.M.–9:24 A.M.
3rd period 9:28 A.M.–10:08 A.M.
4th period 10:12 A.M.–10:52 A.M.
5th period 10:56 A.M.–11:36 A.M.
6th period 11:40 A.M.–12:20 P.M.
7th period 12:24 P.M.–1:04 P.M.
8th period 1:08 P.M.–1:48 P.M.
9th period 1:52 P.M.–2:32 P.M.

Once he saw the specific numbers listed like this, he quickly started remembering which class was in each time slot. For some time slots he drew a blank at first, until he pictured himself leaving the previous class or what kind of books he had to carry, and so on. Within five minutes, he was able to construct the following:

1st period 8:00 A.M.–8:40 A.M. (Woodshop)
2nd period 8:44 A.M.–9:24 A.M. (Woodshop)
3rd period 9:28 A.M.–10:08 A.M. (Swimming/Gym)
4th period 10:12 A.M.–10:52 A.M. (Drafting)

5th period 10:56 A.M.–11:36 A.M. (Algebra)
6th period 11:40 A.M.–12:20 P.M. (Lunch/homeroom)
7th period 12:24 P.M.–1:04 P.M. (English)
8th period 1:08 P.M.–1:48 P.M. (Biology)
9th period 1:52 P.M.–2:32 P.M. (Biology lab)

Lorin was thrilled, because he hadn't thought of that schedule in thirty-five years, and he was amazed that he could bring it back so quickly—and accurately! Armed with this strategy, he then filled in the next three years in a matter of minutes. At one point, he had a block in his junior year, so he went to his former high school's website for clues. After seeing a photo of the auditorium, he remembered that he had a study period following lunch and often slept on one of the uncomfortable hardwood chairs he saw in the photo. (I suppose Lorin's strongest connections to high school stemmed from tardiness and afternoon naps.) Lorin's auditorium/Internet connection is not unusual. Imagine how many resources there are now on the Internet and how all these images and websites can spark all kinds of memories. No memories are gone forever; they are all there waiting to be rediscovered. It's really fun to search and make those connections.

EXERCISE #14: LET YOUR SCHOOL TRACK TAKE YOU BACK

School really does stick with you, whether you realize it or not. So let's use a school track to reconstruct some of your past. For now, let's play with this without paper, just to exercise your mind and memory. Even though you will forget some of it, none of your efforts will be wasted. Think of this as a memory workout.

- Pick a school year that is fairly vivid to you. We are just starting out, so let's keep it at the beginner level for now. If you can't single out one particular year, go for freshman year in high school. That's usually memorable for most of us, because it's full of many first-time moments: a new school, several teachers as opposed to one or two, departmentalization, a big lunchroom, new friends, and new frenemies.
- Try to think of what your schedule was like.
- What was the bus (or car) ride to school like?
- What time did your first class start and what was it?
- Who was your first-period teacher? Try to remember what the room looked like. Try to visualize one of your textbooks.
- Who were some of your friends during that school year? Enemies? Bullies?
- Do you remember any particular projects or memorable events?
- Now try to remember what your second period was and ask yourself the same questions.

Do this same drill for all of your classes. Try to reconstruct your entire freshman class schedule.

For instance, try to remember all of your teachers in ninth grade. Can you remember any of them? What were their names? What classes did they teach? Can you list those classes in order? If you start out following your teacher track, you will probably be able to re-create your entire class schedule. And as you do this, you will be able to retrieve many other memories around the track: your friends' names, your favorite TV shows, how you felt about yourself and others. And in retrieving these memories, you will learn again what you should have retained from your past, all of those little life lessons that you have somehow learned to ignore. In other words, finding one track will help you find others, and before you know it, you'll have reconstructed the story and the memories of your life.

"Everything is connected to everything," Marilu says, and I feel that is certainly true with your brain. There is no isolated path to a memory center of your brain. You can get there probably a million ways by changing your perspective, mood, or manner of thinking. The more you use a track, it seems, the stronger it becomes, and if you can make new connections between memories (using new pathways) then you will eventually find other related memories growing clearer.

—*Alyse Stanley (Marilu.com member)*

Now that you've learned how powerful a track can be in bringing back big chunks of your past, it's time to start logging them and constructing your timeline!

Chapter Six

Organizing and Indexing
Your Memories

The house I grew up in wasn't very large. Eight people, four bedrooms, one bathroom. The room I shared with my oldest sister, JoAnn, was located right off the kitchen, and we had no door, so people in the kitchen could look in and see me sleeping. I was the original *Truman Show*. As you can imagine with a family that big, in a house that small, the place was always a little messy. So I took it upon myself to be the one kid who kept her room clean and organized. It was, after all, constantly on display.

I think my love of show business grew from my room location and the feeling of being constantly watched. My sense of organization was certainly inspired by feeling that my personal space was always in view.

In the little world of my room, everything had to have a place. The tiny closet and dresser I shared with my sister was mine to organize, and I loved making sure each article of clothing was perfectly folded and organized by color and that anything in the closet was hung "like with like" and facing the right way for easy access.

One of my favorite things to do back then, for anyone in the family who asked, was to take something totally chaotic and make sense of it. It didn't matter if it was my mom's jewelry box with tangled necklaces, or a basket of knotted yarn, or even that notoriously messy kitchen drawer. I was there, putting things in their proper locations, after finding the right spot for them in the first place!

It seems logical, then, that my love for remembering can be organized against what is universally known and accepted as the gold standard of date stamping—the calendar. Think about it. What better home for your memories than one that repeats as a reminder for easy reference and repetition? Once I knew I could organize my memories this way, both consciously and unconsciously, I was in. It was like having the perfect backpack for all your school supplies, only this one didn't have to be bought new every year; it was free and available everywhere and at all times . . . in my head!

A big part of memory is organization. No matter how bad a person's memory appears to be, the problem most likely stems from disorganization. It's like the jigsaw puzzle I mentioned in the last chapter, with pieces scattered around your house. All the information is there, but you need a system to piece it all together. It's the same for organizing your autobiographical memory.

From Track to Timeline

Using your main Track and perhaps a few minor tracks, you've already located some big chunks of your past. It's time to organize that information and lay it down on a timeline. Think of your timeline as a giant calendar marking every event of your life, in chronological order. You can use it periodically to review everything you've ever done, analyze it to reveal important behavioral patterns about yourself, or just enjoy it once in a while to get weepy eyed and nostalgic or entertained by the joy of it. Not only will the analysis of your timeline help you take charge of your life, it will also be just plain fun to have at your fingertips. Also, the more you study and analyze it, the more you'll commit it to memory, and that's the circumstance in which autobiographical memory will be most useful to you. The timeline of your life is the "treasure map" to your Total Memory Makeover!

Let's go back to our tracks, using my number one memory student, Lorin (if he's not napping). After he insisted he had a terrible memory (even though he constructed his entire high school schedule in about twenty minutes), I now decided to go after his number one Track, travel! I challenged Lorin to use his travel track to begin construction on his timeline. Without looking at a scrapbook, ticket stub, or diary, he started constructing the following:

1981—06/29/81: Two months—West and East Europe, Russia, Egypt, and Israel 12/06–12/12—Nassau, Bahamas

1982—09/02/82: Three-week drive cross-country: Chicago to L.A., California

1983—07/83: Three-week train trip throughout Peru

1984—07/84: Three-week train trip throughout Japan

1985—No trip that year

1986—4/02/86: Two months Australia, New Zealand, and Hawaii

1987—07/87: Three weeks—France, Holland, Italy, Switzerland

1988—01/88: Two weeks—Las Vegas, Salt Lake City, and Phoenix

1989—No trip that year

1990—06/90: France, Italy, Greece, Turkey, and England

1991—08/91: Cross-country drive—Chicago to L.A., Route 90

1992—06/92: Cross-country drive—L.A. to Chicago, Route 10 and Route 40

1993

1994

1995—04/95: Cross-country drive—L.A. to Chicago, Interstate 10 through New Orleans

1996—Summer '96: Mexico City, Teotihuacan, and Puebla

1997—August '97: France, Poland, Belarus, Czech Republic, and Slovakia

1998

1999

2000—August '00: China—Beijing, Xian, Shanghai, Yangtze River cruise

2001—09/20: Paris, Rome

2002—05/07: Ireland

2003

2004—07/10: Japan and China

2005

2006—08/06: Ukraine, Hungary, Romania, Italy

2007—08/31: South Africa, Botswana, Zambia, Malawi, Tanzania, and Kenya

2008—06/08: Vietnam, Cambodia, Thailand

2009

2010—10/14: Cross-country drive—Los Angeles to New York

2011

2012

This is how Lorin's timeline looked after only fifteen minutes. He then continued filling in the years in the same fashion, until he had something written for every year right up to the present, 2012.

Once he had all the years filled in, I guided him to go back and fill in each trip in more detail. He started with his 1981 Europe trip.

Summer two-month Eurail Youth Pass trip
06/29/81: Left JFK New York to Gatwick London
07/03/81: Arnhem, Holland
07/06/81: Berlin, West Germany
07/09/81: Warsaw, Poland
07/12/81: Moscow, USSR
07/15/81: Leningrad, USSR
07/17/81: Helsinki, Finland
07/19/81: Stockholm, Sweden
07/21/81: Hamburg, West Germany
07/23/81: Zermatt, Switzerland
07/26/81: Venice, Italy
07/29/81: Athens, Greece
07/31/81: Jerusalem, Israel
08/03/81: Cairo, Egypt
08/08/81: Luxor, Egypt
08/11/81: Aswan, Egypt
08/12/81: Rome, Italy
08/15/81: Pisa, Italy
08/16/81: Nice, France
08/22/81: Barcelona, Spain
08/26/81: Paris, France
08/30/81: London, England
08/31/81: Flight home to New York

Reconstructing a trip from thirty years ago to the precise dates and locations was more amazing to Lorin than his reconstruction of his entire high school schedule. Unlike the school schedule, he did this without any outside help—receipts, photos, scrapbook, Internet, or phone-a-friend. Plus he thoroughly enjoyed all the images that came flooding back while doing this, and he even donned a French beret for some parts and did a little Greek table dancing for others. His incredulity was conquered, and I explained to him that this was possible because travel is his main Track.

Lorin claims he does not have superior autobiographical memory. When people ask him if he has it (as I do), he jokes, "No, I chose X-ray vision instead." Lorin has lots of special talents, but SAM isn't one of them. (Or as he says, "SAM I am not!") Yet he was able to remember what he was doing every day for a two-month stretch thirty years ago! And he now realizes he can do this for every trip he has taken since. He can also tell you what he was doing in the weeks and months leading up to all of his trips. All of this information creates a great foundation for his remembering everything else.

Building and Organizing Your Personal Timeline

It is now time to expand your timeline from the micro to the macro version, from laying down one track to laying down lots of tracks on your timeline. After Lorin laid down his school and travel tracks, he laid down his job track, then his sports track, then his holiday track, and so on.

Now that you know how to do it, let's talk about how and where you should build this timeline. Perhaps the easiest way to construct your timeline is in an online document. You can also use a good old notebook and pen, but that will become more difficult to organize as you add more and more entries. The good thing about using a word processing program is that it can automatically organize each entry by date. You can also build your timeline at a website specifically designed for this purpose (a quick search will yield several).

Here is an example of how I would input dates, using a birthdays-and-weddings track:

4/6/1952—My birthday
5/12/1994—My son Nick's birthday
11/12/1995—My son Joey's birthday
9/28/1980—My first marriage, to Frederic Forrest
7/10/1990—My second marriage, to Robert Lieberman
12/21/2006—My third marriage, to Michael Brown
?/?/20??—My fourth marriage, to . . . Only kidding! Imagine
   how long this marriage list would have taken Elizabeth
   Taylor.

Begin each entry in your list with the date so that you can later use the "sort" function to put them in chronological order.

The entries in your list will automatically be sorted chronologically like this:

4/6/1952—My birthday
9/28/1980—My first marriage, to Frederic Forrest
6/27/1990—My second marriage, to Robert Lieberman
5/12/1994—My son Nick's birthday
11/12/1995—My son Joey's birthday
12/21/2006—My third marriage, to Michael Brown

Once you establish the pattern and know how to input dates and events, just add to your timeline as you please, as much or as little as you want. All you have to do is lead with a date for each of the memories you've retrieved from your track or archives. If Lorin, for example, input all of the dates from his trips, they would automatically be sorted chronologically with every other date. When you're not sure of a date, just estimate, so it will be placed close to where it should go. Once you have matched each item to its place on your timeline, it will be there forever to be retrieved when needed. As I said, you can make this as simple or as complex and detailed as you want, but it shouldn't take more than a couple of seconds to input each entry.

Your timeline is an ongoing process, and within this process, you will be continually adding information. Don't be surprised if your passion to add more intensifies as your timeline grows. This can be very addictive. It's like Facebook, where the more friends you uncover from the past, the more you want to find. The more you document about yourself, the more insights you will have, and this will inspire you to find more. This exercise is about having fun and giving yourself a chance to get an overview of your life in a way that not many people ever do.

Even if you only dabble part-time in your memory makeover for three weeks and then stop, you will already notice an increase in your autobiographical memory aptitude and, no doubt, develop a new appreciation for your past. You will start living more con-sciously, because you'll become aware of things that have been influencing your life every day, both positives and negatives, as con-nections are made. This exercise is essential to your Total Memory Makeover, because it works parts of your brain that you may have never deliberately used before. Like a muscle, the more you exer-cise your memory, the stronger it becomes. And you can exercise it as often—or not—as you like. Being a calendar girl, I always feel that knowing the years, months, or even specific days wherein your track lies will help you uncover other important days, including cur-rent events. And being able to identify these other incidents will help you connect with memories long forgotten.

THE GIFT OF TIME(LINE)

One of my favorite gifts to give someone (besides organizing their closet!) is a timeline of something from our relationship. In 2010, when Lorin moved back to New York after having lived in Los Angeles for nineteen years, I sat down and fired off a log of some of our best times during his years here. In one sitting I filled six solid single-spaced pages of listings, and this action is what inspired many of the memory-prompting exercises you see in this book. Earlier that year, I had also given as a birthday gift to my ex-husband Rob a list of how we've celebrated his birthday for the past twenty-five years. This is what these lists looked like:

SOME OF THE ENTRIES FOR LORIN'S GOING-AWAY GIFT:

19910325—Visit to LA

19910906—Arrival in LA to live

19911117—Made dinner in apt for Rob and me

19911213—Include Me Out! at USC followed by dinner at Ca'Brea

19911225—Chicago Xmas

19920412–19920419—Cal a Vie (fans, classes, massages, heart beeping)

19920418—Holy Saturday break-in by Kirk at house averted by John the ex-marine

19920420—Move to Hilton for the week

19920429–19920430—LA Riots (Armed guard and Rob's Riot Soup)

19920514—14th, 15th, & 18th Dancerobics shoot

19920515—Ate at Il Mito after Friday shoot and pigged out!

19920728—Trial for Kirk

19920801—Lloyd's wedding (sat w/Johnny and Kelly)

19921005—Week of promos for Dancerobics in NY (Joan Rivers, Regis and Kathie Lee)

19921200—Aspen updates all month

19921220—Leave for Aspen

19921221—First day on slopes

19921225—Xmas on Friday

19921231—New Year's Eve at the Jerome

19930102—Everyone leaves

19931222—Everyone in Tonight Show audience followed by big party at house

19931225—Xmas L.A.

19931231—R & I in Aspen, Ls in Chicago

19940512—Nicky's birth

19940604—4th, 5th, 6th of June—Marilu Show pilots

19940712—Marilu Show starts production

19941012—Surprise Family Show

19941218—Sunday—Aspen

19941225—Sunday—Aspen

19950128—We went to the Golden Globes!

19950201—Wednesday—Grease Reunion Show—Farfalla night

19950714—Friday night at Farfalla (Nicky got locked in car and busboys got him out)

19951112—Joey born!

AND HERE IS SOME OF ROB'S BIRTHDAY GIFT (THE DATE, HIS BIRTHDAY, JULY 16, WAS ALWAYS THE SAME):

1990—Monday—In LA. We were recently married. You had left France on July 11, the day after Christal & Roy's wedding, to start Gabriel's Fire. I had gone to Italy with some of the family and left them to come and be with you on your birthday. We went to Patina to celebrate.

1991—Tuesday—In LA. You were in the middle of All I Want for Christmas and I was shooting Noises Off. Lorne and I cooked dinner for you and we ate out on the balcony. Chocolate mousse from the Nowhere Café. Great meal!

1992—Thursday—In LA. Great evening. Big party out on deck with family and friends. Watched Clinton accept nomination and then greeted guests. Lorin gave you microphone. Your mom's speech . . . "I work alone, Marilu."

1993—Friday—In LA. Celebrated night before at Patina because I shot Evening Shade *the night of your birthday. The entire cast and audience sang "Happy Birthday" to you.*

1994—Saturday—In LA. Went to see afternoon showing of Forrest Gump *leaving Nicky with that oddball nanny for the first and only time. Donna had left on Thursday right before we went to see* The Sisters Rozenzweig *and I was distraught. You kept saying, "It's okay. We get to keep the baby!"*

1995—Sunday—In Minneapolis. Nicky and I left on the Friday the 14th after celebrating your birthday with the cast and crew at lunch on your set. You on roller skates and Nicky doing the Dionne Farris song "I Know." The morning of your birthday, MaryAnn and David (who were living downstairs) made you breakfast and set out the cutout of Nicky and me that your prop guy made of us.

1996—Tuesday—In Vancouver. My favorite of all times! Celebrated at dinner with Joan Harrison from CBS on the day, but on Saturday, I surprised you with the boat ride and full sushi bar for you, David, MaryAnn and me. Incredible, unforgettable night!

1997—Wednesday—In NYC. I was doing Chicago *and Bob Carney and Cynthia (his wife) were in town and came to see the show. After the show, fourteen of us went to Picholine to celebrate your birthday.*

1998—Thursday—In LA. We celebrated the day after with a huge group of people in the private room at Il Sole because you were out of town on your actual birthday.

1999—Friday—In Las Vegas. Night before at the China Grill with Erin, Trent, and Cheslow. That night JFK Jr.'s plane went down. On Saturday we celebrated your birthday at our house in Henderson during the day with a big barbecue before my two shows (Chicago) that night. Sad news on TV all day.

2000—Sunday—I was in NYC rehearsing Annie Get Your Gun, so we celebrated when you came to join us a week later in Dallas at Benihana. The boys loved it!

Sifting Through Your Personal Archives

After inputting dates from your main tracks and your most important personal events, try retrieving memories and possibly specific dates for your timeline from objects all around you. If you can't think of the specific date, estimate. When I ask people to remember an event from their past, like their twenty-first birthday, a graduation, Christmas, or a wedding, they usually start recalling two or three big moments from the event. They'll say something like, "I remember going to dinner with my family at the Town and Country restaurant, then coming home afterward and having cake in the living room." When I ask them to tell me more details, I'll hear responses like, "No, that's about it. I just don't remember any more." Or "I seem to have a block to the rest of what happened that night." People only remember a few highlights from past events, because those are the moments that flash in their mind whenever that event is brought up. It is sort of the default thumbnail image that pops up to represent that event.

Try it yourself to see what I mean. Think of an event from your past, like your high school graduation. If you're like most people, you might remember the friends and relatives who came to witness and celebrate with you, a moment or two from the ceremony, some of your classmates and things they said to you, an image of how you looked in your cap and gown, and perhaps one or two other moments. People usually remember only brief moments and feelings, especially if it has been several decades since the event.

Now imagine how much more you would remember from that day if you were able to look at the graduation program and compare notes with your other classmates and share each other's photographs and videos. Think of the "Memory Block" and "Memory Partner Prompting" exercises you did in chapter 4. Each object you bring into this process sparks more and more memories that you either completely forgot or remembered inaccurately. It's like Lorin's seeing the hard wooden chairs from his high school auditorium online; it sparked memories of how he behaved in that space—mainly napping.

Fortunately, you are surrounded by these material memory prompts without even going online. Practically every object in your home contains memories that can help you reconstruct your past. Photos, videos, receipts, bank statements, notebooks, and school-work all bear notations or clues as to when, why, and how you acquired them. Like Lorin seeing the auditorium photo, objects and other hard evidence can augment your tracks and help you access random memories. That's why you probably keep so many of them—as *mementos*—and why people who keep scrapbooks and photo albums often refer to them as "memory books." Did you know that "souvenir" means "to remember" in French? Most of us intuitively understand that our belongings help preserve memories, and that those memories are worth preserving.

Marilu and I met in 1981 when my husband, her business manager, introduced us, because he thought we would really like each other and I could help her "get dressed." It was love at first sight. Well, I got past what she was wearing, and we became best friends, and I became one of the few people allowed in her OCD-like closet. There, I revisited every romance and man she has ever dated, kissed, starred with, wanted to star with, wanted to kiss . . . Well, you get the drift, right? They all had two things in common: They all wanted to buy clothes for that beautiful body of hers, and they were not stylists. Needless to say, we have kept many unnecessary clothing items that have many fantastic stories behind them—stories that, sadly, are too salacious for this book.

—*Sharon Feldstein*

Of course, everybody has a different method for storing the "stuff" of their lives. Some people want to get rid of the evidence as soon as possible; others can't seem to part with anything. Most of us fit somewhere in between. So pick a drawer, cabinet, box, or closet that you've been meaning to clean and organize. Memory retrieval provides a perfect opportunity to kill two birds with one stone. And the fun part about this project is that so many items in an unorganized drawer full of . . . well . . . *anything* can provide hundreds of memory prompts for events long forgotten.

As soon as you start sorting through it, you'll know exactly what I mean: A dentist's appointment card tells you when you last had your teeth cleaned. Receipts from Home Depot mark the day you painted the family room, and airline ticket receipts tell you when you went to Atlanta. Bank statements and receipts not only reveal lots of forgotten treasures; they also provide accurate dates of hundreds of events. And with photographs and videos, you can really explore your perceptions and feelings from the past and compare them to how you see and feel things today. Your archives will help you fill in many blanks in your timeline.

Three years ago I decided to take all the photos in our house and organize them in chronological order. I'm a big one for grouping things "like with like," so I bought various-sized photo boxes in order to have a place for each image, without having different-sized pictures lumped together. Some of the photos had the date already on them (and some wrong dates, at that), but most had nothing noted, so it was up to my memory to date and file them correctly. After tackling the photos and filling sixteen boxes with four-by-six photographs, and eight large tubs with eight-by-tens and other various-sized images, I then moved on to our family videos (going back to 1985!). I fast-forwarded through each one and knew exactly when each was shot, without the date's being on the screen. Talk about a trip down memory lane! Once the system was in place, it's been easy to keep it up. To this day, I know exactly where to go to find any image or video. My family's archival history is all organized and ready to go for any school project or memory prompting anyone needs.

Meta-Tagging Your Memories

Your goal is to continue filling in this enormous timeline of your life. Keep in mind that every entry and date can be sparked from several categories, or meta-tags: your main Track, tickets, receipts, career and school items, souvenirs, friends, and the Internet. Memories are not bound to only one path of retrieval. I refer to these as meta-tags because meta-tags are like search words on the Internet that may be different, but they are all connected to the same root subject. A Gawker article about gourmet food trucks might be tagged with "New York," "food trends," "street vendors," and so on. This allows Google to find the data based upon clues given to it through the search bar. Each day is such a full and distinct experience that if you decided to meta-tag it, you would have an endless list of characteristics to help define and locate that day. You can do it by what you ate, what you wore, where you worked, or where you lived; you could use current events to "tag" a day, or personal events like your age, your child's age, the standing of your baseball team, the length of your hair. The way we recognize each day in our past reveals how our mind has meta-tagged that day.

Keep in mind that our brains take in information and then store it using tags that help us retrieve it later, without our even realizing it. These tags tend to run along our tracks. I know this all sounds unbelievably complicated, because it is! Memory and the brain are so complex; much of their inner workings are still a mystery. But don't be intimidated by that or bogged down with its complexity—focus more on enjoying the ride. Just remember that our brains code and store information by attaching it to related information already on our hard drives, so one key to retrieving a memory is to identify other recollections that share its common tags. For example, if you're trying to remember a word in English, you might review words with similar meanings in Latin, French, or Italian, but you wouldn't think of searching words with the same meaning in Chinese. Why? Because English, French, and Italian share roots stemming from Latin, but Chinese doesn't. The same principle applies when recalling memories: Consider their roots and let those roots guide you to memories related to the one you're trying to retrieve. With memories, the common tags might be the year or season when an event occurred, the people who were there, the age of your kids or parents at the time, the emotional tenor of the event, and the time of day, just to name a few. Even if you can't recall the particulars of a moment, you likely have a vague sense of it. That vague sense will contain the common tags your brain has used to store the memory. Use those tags to identify the cluster of memories associated with the one you're trying to remember, and that cluster will help you zero in on your target.

EXERCISE #15: USING META-TAGGING

Here's a fun way to show the power of common tags for eliciting memories. Divide a piece of paper into four columns. Label the columns with the following titles: 1. Hot Weather, 2. Cold Weather, 3. Rainstorms, 4. Snowstorms. (People in Southern California could label these as 1. Over 70°, 2. Under 70°, 3. Foggy Days, 4. Trips to Aspen. If you're from Minnesota, try 1. Above Freezing, 2. Below Freezing, 3. Blizzards, 4. Really *Bad* Blizzards.)

Now see how many days/events you can recall for each of those four weather categories in the next ten minutes. Work quickly and don't go over the time limit. Using once again my favorite memory student, Lorin, the following are his results for this exercise:

HOT WEATHER
a. Beach day with the Puchtas in August 1977
b. Cubs baseball game with Chuck Hall and Steve Hager, 1966
c. Second-class train ride in Vietnam, June 2008
d. Day at the U.S. Open, New York, September 2010
e. Unbearable mosquitoes at Nippersink Resort, June 1976

COLD WEATHER
f. Delivering law bulletin in downtown Chicago, January 1973
g. Ice-skating at Haas Park, December 1969

h. Sledding in Lincoln Park followed by hot chocolate, January 1971
i. Stuck on a ski lift in Snowmass, December 1992
j. Walking with canvas shoes in Segovia, Spain, in January 2010

RAINSTORMS

k. Thunderstorm in Washington, DC, National Mall, August 2009
l. Unusual orange-colored hue in backyard in Chicago, 1967
m. Monsoon in Phnom Penh, Cambodia, June 2008

SNOWSTORMS

n. Blizzard as backdrop for flamenco show, New York, January 2011
o. April blizzard in Chicago, 1975
p. Washington, DC, blizzard, January 1996
q. February blizzard, Chicago, 1967

Hopefully, by doing this exercise, you brought back a few images you haven't thought about for a long time, and you were able to add more dates and entries to your timeline. Using weather as a common denominator can bring up lots of memories scattered randomly over several decades, because they are linked by very memorable conditions. This can be done with other common tags, as well.

Try lots of these meta-tags to retrieve and input more into your timeline. If you've used all the retrieval tools we've discussed so far, you should have a fairly extensive timeline by now.

At this point, you must be thinking, "What should I do now?"

Chapter Seven

Better Learning Through Memory

$\mathcal{M}$emory is the diary that we all carry about with us.

—*Oscar Wilde*

$\mathcal{I}$n this chapter you are going to be using your timeline to start a diary to analyze the most important and most revealing moments in your life. Now is your chance to start a journal that will really tell a story. Make it your goal to freely and truthfully express your feelings and insights. Think about your relationships with partners, family, and friends, and patterns (negative and positive) that repeat frequently. Analyze your relationships with food and money and habits and addictions. Many connections can be made when you are brave enough to look honestly at your past and connect the dots. You should also, of course, note the times you felt your best and what you may have done to influence that particular outcome. There's nothing like reading about past success to compel you to feel that way again. This diary can be used as a tool for reflection, by comparing it to the memories gleaned from your timeline. It can also be used for connecting your past to the present you live each day.

Thursday, May 20, 1982

I left for an eight-week trip around the world that started with the Cannes Film Festival. Having kept a diary on and off since I was fourteen, I decided this was another perfect time to keep one, not only because I was visiting new places, but also because I was going to be away from my therapist, the brilliant Dr. Ruth Velikovsky Sharon (with whom I later wrote the book *I Refuse to Raise a Brat*). I had been in psychoanalysis for seven years at that point, and it had completely changed my life. When people asked why I started psychoanalysis at twenty-three years old, I always explained, "Why wait to be an old, wise person?" Like Socrates, I have always believed that "the unexamined life is not worth living."

Dr. Sharon was not only my therapist; she was also working with my husband at the time, the talented and complicated Frederic Forrest. Freddie and I had met on the set of the film *Hammett,* fell in love, and got married, and we were off to France, because the film was in competition at the 1982 Cannes Film Festival. Our short, tumultuous marriage had been a roller coaster to be sure, and we were now embarking on an around-the-world tour throughout Europe and Asia to really test our union. We lasted only ten days in France before finding ourselves arguing on a street corner on the Left Bank of Paris, realizing a break was necessary to sort it all out. He left for Bangkok and a movie shoot, and I made a plan to join him the following week, after we had both cooled down.

So there I was. No husband. No therapy. No language (except broken high school French). Tons of feelings. And only my diary to help me sort it all out.

I had started a typical "Dear Diary, today I . . ." daily journal on the plane to Nice, but at this point of my trip, I knew more than ever that tracking every emotion and insight was more important than describing every meal and tourist trap. Besides, knowing I was in for a rough time with my marriage, I wanted to be able to share my day-to-day emotional journey with Dr. Sharon when I returned, and I could only do this through a journal. So at the top of each page, I listed chronologically what I did throughout the day, like a to-do list, but my nitty-gritty gut-spilling entries were saved for when I was sitting on trains, sipping a Campari on a piazza, or looking out over the Mediterranean.

Ah, yes! Big change of plans. After leaving Freddie on that street corner in Paris, I found myself—through a series of coincidences—spending three weeks traveling throughout Italy, which changed my entire life. To this day, I call this journal my Italian Diary, even though Italy was not originally a stop on my around-the-world tour! In fact, during the eight weeks I spent traveling, there were very few Plan A aspects to the entire trip. It was Plan B all the way, as I found myself meeting up with a friend in Genoa; spending a week in Naples; and taking a four A.M. train up to Rome, where I was supposed to get on a plane to Bangkok but instead met a porter who invited me to spend ten days in the country with his wife and family before I took a side trip to Munich, where I caught a plane (finally) to Bangkok to meet up with Freddie. Our final two weeks together were spent deciding to get a divorce and taking off to Hong Kong for one last fling.

On the flight coming home, I reread my diary. The plane could have been fueled solely by the lightbulbs going off in my head. I could see in my writing exactly the specific issues I needed to focus on when I got back into therapy, especially the issues and decisions concerning my marriage and career. By stepping back, observing, documenting, and analyzing my life, for maybe the first time, I could see it objectively. It was almost as if I could give sound advice to myself as a caring best friend would because I was reading it all in one shot rather than living it in the moment and accepting whatever was happening. We can often see what's best for our friends and family, but we don't always see what is best for ourselves, even if the choices are obvious. One of the main reasons my Italian trip was a real eye-opener for me was that I was forced to communicate with people in a language I didn't know, making it imperative for me to simplify everything. I could observe others and pick up the nuances of their tone, rather than being influenced by their words, and vice versa. Because I couldn't rely on any irony or verbal razzle-dazzle to get my point across, I had to slow down and really bottom-line my intentions. Sitting on that plane, I filled in the remaining pages with my newfound knowledge, having looked at my past mistakes and triumphs in black and white. You can imagine how many diary pages I read to Dr. Sharon when I was back on the couch in New York!

My Italian Diary was a tremendous breakthrough for me because it illustrated in black and white what was important to me—everything from what I really wanted in a marriage, to food and body issues, to my realizing how words have little to do with communication. But my diary wouldn't have been a breakthrough had I not been making a conscious effort to remember so much from my past prior to that trip. I was able to make connections that were not obvious to me before, because I was taking the time to reflect on not only what I was doing then, but also how it was linked to my previous behaviors. It's one thing to be able to objectively analyze your life, but if you're only working with recent information, you're not clearly seeing the whole picture. The more data you have regarding your past, the better you can understand your current circumstances and direction. To this day, I review my Italian Diary, along with the various diaries I have written throughout my life, not only because I get to revisit a fabulous trip, but I also get to make new connections and insights into my past.

The Importance of Intention and Reflection Goals

The more connections that can be made in the brain, the more integrated the experience is within memory.

—*Don Campbell*

Before you actually begin your diary, there are a few things to consider. First of all, you have to recognize that developing your memory takes continued effort, especially if you truly want a Total Memory Makeover. You have to discipline yourself enough to say, "Okay, this is what I'm going for. This is what I really want to change and what I'd really like to remember." You need to determine your focus and decide what you want to recapture, analyze, and discover about yourself. Embrace the challenge of making mental notes throughout your day, and keep your diary with you, so you won't miss opportunities to express yourself. You must fully immerse yourself in the mind-set of remembering and analyzing your past, while paying attention to the lessons within.

To get the most out of the fabulous timeline you've created, examine what was going on beneath the immediate emotional surface of the entries. For example, let's say you've written, "First date with so and so," and with that, you can remember that during that dinner, as sexy and flirtatious as it was, there were red flags (their being inconsiderate, short-tempered, self-centered, cheap, or so on) that you failed to recognize at the time. But in retrospect, and with a newfound awareness, you are determined to never let a red flag like that go unnoticed again during a date. Or let's say you know you have money issues but never wanted to face them head-on, out of fear of being overwhelmed and paralyzed should you really recognize the truth. Looking at your timeline, you notice that every January, you've started the year in debt, but with good intentions. But by July, you are bored with being frugal, and you're looking for your next purchase. And why not? You've been good for six months, and now everything is on sale. So there you go again, making the same mistakes by not foreseeing the debt you'll be in by the time the holidays roll around again.

Only through intention and reflection can we recognize the patterns of our past as a key to understanding our current life and behavior. Knowing the broad strokes of your past, which patterns of behavior are you hoping to discover in yourself? What has prevented you from changing what you truly want to change and avoiding making the same mistakes over and over again? However, you can't just go through the motions and expect success. To be useful, memory requires direction and a sense of purpose. You have to mindfully make the effort to plan what you're going to do, do it, and then think about what you just did. In other words, don't forget about APR: *anticipation, participation,* and *recollection*! It's a never-ending process. But it's a process that becomes second nature after a while, just as living a healthier lifestyle becomes instinctive, once you get the hang of it. I know this makeover sounds like a lot of homework, but hang in there. Once you get on a roll with it, your life will get a lot easier. You won't spend all your time second-guessing the same mistakes; it will all be there in black and white.

The Most Important Chapters of Your Life

You are almost ready to begin your diary. But before analyzing your timeline and making notations in your diary/journal, it's best to organize it into chapters. Don't worry, this should only take a few minutes. In order to see it more clearly, your timeline should eventually read like the table of contents of a book or the outline of a script. It's difficult to make sense of your entire life when seeing it all at once, so in this step, you put in dividers. By dividing your timeline into sections, it becomes more digestible and it'll be easier to identify and understand patterns. After all, you can't judge what you did in your teens by the same standards as your adult life. To find your chapters, imagine that you are about to write your biography or produce an A & E documentary about yourself. You may have already fantasized about how your life would play out as a movie or book, and in doing so, your first assignment would be to create chapters. This is actually fun and interesting to do! Think about what have been the most significant segments of your life. There is no exact formula for this; it's how you see it. Most people choose between eight and fifteen chapters, but feel free to do more or less. Using your timeline, try to determine where you would place your divisions between chapters.

Here are some other things to consider when dividing these segments on your timeline:

1. Places you've lived
2. Schools
3. Jobs
4. Family events
5. Relationships
6. Marriages
7. Deaths
8. Divorces
9. Vacations
10. Pets
11. Spiritual experiences
12. Important realizations

13. Mentors
14. Important friends
15. Challenging rivalries

I've had my biography on three networks (A & E, Lifetime, and E!), and when they divided my life for television profiles, it was more or less done like this:

1. Early life
2. Father's death
3. *Grease*
4. Broadway
5. Mother's death
6. *Taxi*
7. Discovering health
8. Marriage to Freddie
9. Films
10. Marriage to Rob
11. *Evening Shade*
12. Nick and Joey
13. Back to Broadway (*Chicago*)
14. Writing books (getting on the *New York Times* best-seller list!)
15. Divorce from Rob
16. Marriage to Michael
17. *60 Minutes* and HSAM

What were the most significant events in your life? Often these provide pivotal/transitional moments when our lives change direction. For example, my father's death was a huge turning point for my family and me, because so much of our life changed after that tragic event. Change is not always obvious as it happens, but looking back years later, it's possible to see how our lives and behaviors are significantly altered after certain events. Friday, November 22, 1963, the day President Kennedy was shot, is a good example of a chapter divider for the timeline of the United States. Many historians believe American innocence was lost on that day. The events of 9/11 would, of course, be another big marker on our history's timeline and that date is considered a huge turning point for the world.

What are the big markers on *your* timeline? I can look at each entry on my list and instantly recognize the changes that took place from it. I know at a glance what action I took to either shore up or remedy the momentum of each turn of events, whether it was recovering from the pain of loss or setting up my life to support something wonderful.

Diary Time

Once you've got your life divided into chapters, take a good look. Think about everything already discussed throughout the preceding chapters: relationships, feelings, mistakes, triumphs, goals, dreams, needs, strengths, weaknesses, and any obvious connections. Now it's time to start writing in your diary. Don't edit and don't hold back. Let it all out. Whenever you slow down or hit a roadblock, go back and study your timeline. Don't feel you have to do all this in one sitting, of course. Let your inspiration guide you. Take all the time you need, and don't worry much about structure; just let it flow. You can even list bullet points to be filled in later. Pretend you are speaking to a psychoanalyst, and fill in as many pages as you need to express yourself. You may, in fact, need to start a second journal just hours after filling up the first one, especially if you've been waiting a long time to get all of these feelings out.

Keep an eye on patterns and their meaning and significance to what you've written. What from your past could be connected to what you are currently doing? This question is especially significant if you are experiencing an underlying feeling of stress lately. Something may not be metabolizing well in your system, and it is either an effect of the stress or a cause of it. Think about your triggers. What has caused stress in the past? Is it connected to what you're feeling today? Ask yourself things like, "Why haven't I been able to conquer this problem so far? What needs to be resolved?"

At this point, aim to identify problems, analyze their cause, and try to work toward a solution. You are looking at your past, because that is usually where the problems and solutions live. Ask yourself, "What have been the typical circumstances when I find it difficult to express myself? Is this similar to anything I'm experiencing today? Whose feelings am I protecting, and why have I habitually been doing that? What usually sets off this emotional trigger?" When you locate the problem, think of options to solve it. For example, if you need to confront someone about something that's been eating away at you, can you confront that person honestly but diplomatically? You may come to the realization that you're being too judgmental and you need to step back a bit. Perhaps you need to incorporate more stress management in your life, like exercise or meditation, to release tension and get more sleep. At the end of the day, you may still have the problem, but at least you'll know that you are actively doing something about it, which is moving you toward a solution.

One of my memory students spent years picking the wrong guy. She had complained constantly that "the good ones are not available" or "the wrong ones" seemed to pick her or "the bad boys are sexier." (We've all been there!) She'd go on her first date, tell people about it, and they'd tell her, "Oh no! Here we go again!" But she'd ignore the signs and think, *No. This time is different. He's not like that. And I don't even want to think about my ex!* It wasn't until her intensive memory work going over her past relationships that she started looking at her complete dating history. She was finally willing to connect the dots of her past to see a clearer picture of her present. She started taking responsibility for choosing the wrong guys, and she finally found the right one!

Anyone who has read any of my past books knows that a big struggle for me was my weight and food choices. I can remember plenty of mornings in the early seventies that were reminiscent of Martin Sheen in *Apocalypse Now:* "Saigon . . . Sh**! I'm still only in Saigon." Only my protest was, "Fat! Damn it, I'm still fat!" It was this big dark cloud I had to face every day. But once I took a good hard look at myself and accepted my reality, it compelled me to discover a better way of eating and to get control of my weight. I have never forgotten the feelings I had when I was struggling with it, imprisoned emotionally and physically in a body that made me unhappy and unhealthy. I could never go back to that old way of eating *now*, because I continually remember how bad it felt *then*.

After my parents died and I took action to learn everything I could about the human body and food, I realized that there was no excuse for my staying heavy and unhealthy. It began to feel selfish that here I was educating myself so thoroughly about nutrition, yet I couldn't stop struggling with food and body issues, thereby keeping me from sharing with others all of my newfound knowledge. I started to make a list of all the reasons I caved when faced with the decision to give in or be good and came up with the thirty-three ways I was self-sabotaging at any given crossroad. Besides loving the social aspects of eating, many of the triggers had to do with control, or lack thereof. Once I identified this issue, I was able to flash back to the times in my life when I'd put on a lot of weight because I felt out of my element or couldn't relate to the people with whom I was working. Making this connection with my past, I was finally able to stop myself from acting out with food.

When you truly connect with a memory that made you unhappy, you can feel it down to your bones. One of the reasons this lesson takes so long to learn is because we naturally try to get away with as much as we can. We go back and forth, hoping to control our temptations. It's easy to think we can indulge "part-time." We're like Dr. Jekyll, unable to fully get rid of Mr. Hyde, because we secretly want to have that wilder side, separate from our guilt-ridden, disciplined side.

When we were in the memory class with Marilu, she brought me back to the place when my health was at its worst. By the specific questions she asked, I could see myself going through the motions of a binging/purging weekend. I saw myself in my little yellow Escape in the drive-through of Jack in the Box and then going to Safeway for the ice cream and chips, and the boxes of laxatives. I could taste the laxatives and I remember the feeling of how I was going to throw up before I would get the amount of laxatives down (which would be between fifty to sixty). As the memories came flooding back, I could see how my face looked in the mirror the morning after a night of hell.

The memory continued as I thought of how Wild Oats smelled the next day, because I had made a vow to myself that I was going to get healthy. Thank God that day in the book section I found Marilu's *30-Day Total Health Makeover!*

—*Kecia Newton (Marilu.com member)*

In addition to overeating, take a look at other struggles and addictions. Smoking is still a big one for some people, and it's a good example of how we can continue to flirt with something even though we know it's ultimately making us unhappy. Smokers are always trying to find new ways to smoke without giving it up completely. They'll try to limit themselves to only smoking three cigarettes a day, or only on weekends or vacations, or only after meals, or just low-tar cigarettes. It becomes a game of "How much can I get away with while still feeling like I'm in control?" They keep trying different ways to beat it, but it takes over their lives until they finally realize there is only one solution: giving up cigarettes completely and for good! It's the same with drinking, overeating, cheating, gambling, choosing the wrong partner, and everything else that is potentially addictive. We love to walk to the edge! We love to see how much we can get away with before we really have to shape up. It becomes a question of "How much can I tease and tempt and take myself way out there before I have to pay for my destructive behavior?" Put another way, "What's my tolerance level for the discomfort of feeling bad the next day?"

I can truly say that my commitment to journaling and analyzing my past demons has helped me conquer them for good. Look for the same types of clues (didn't get enough sleep, ate my feelings, didn't speak up for myself, didn't take chances, lack of preparation, and so on) in your timeline. Think of what you were doing at each entry. How did you feel? Who was involved? Think of the positive moments, as well. The opposite of the spectrum works the same way. When you spot a great day on your timeline, think of the same questions. What made that day so wonderful? What guided you in the right direction? Was it just luck? Or did you earn that particular reward? When you think of a past graduation day, does it make you proud, because you worked hard to reach that finish line? Or do you wish you worked harder for grades that would have made you even prouder? Think about that day in high school when you really studied hard for a test or an assignment and you were on top of your game. You felt great, because your performance was great.

Are you seeing any painful Ghosts of Christmas Past? Perhaps you realize you've been overly sensitive to reactions from others. Perhaps this stems from being ignored or overly protected by your parents. There's nothing wrong with this. Don't be afraid to ask these kinds of questions. If you give yourself over to this process, you will begin to make connections and understand much of your own behavior and see lots of things you've been missing. That's when you can begin to change what you want to change. You learn to reinforce the good and avoid repeating the bad. It's a very exciting place to be.

Looking back helps you see those around you more clearly, as well. Perhaps you discover that your father or mother was habitually stressed or tired or angry, or that you grew up with a sibling who bullied or belittled you. Every important encounter in the past should beg the question, "What is this similar to in the present?"

When I was about ten (1966), my mom took me shopping for summer clothes. She was so mad because the capris I picked out were exactly the same as my best friend's. She wanted me to be my own person. From the time my daughter was very little, I have always told her, "Be your own person." Just maybe, I learned that from my mom . . . way back when. Connections, connections.

—*Jill Nelson*

LEGACY QUESTIONNAIRE

I have always been fascinated with the subject of legacy and how our being raised a certain way impacts the choices we make every day. Are we causing our own problems by ignoring the warning signs? Do we often set up certain types of situations because they make us feel comfortably uncomfortable? Are we choosing the people we choose because our place in the family attracts us to people who "complete" us the same way? What is inherent in the cultural legacy (heritage, family, socioeconomic level) of each of us?

I have listed questions regarding what I consider to be the five most basic areas that cover legacy. There are so many others, but I think it's best to focus on just these five in order to best understand our past and help to positively predict and shape our future.

YOUR FAMILY IN THE COMMUNITY/NEIGHBORHOOD
Think back to your childhood and answer these questions:

1. Get an image of your family when you were growing up and its place in your neighborhood/community. How would you define it? Please reflect on why.
    a. Big fish, little pond
    b. Little fish, big pond
    c. Little fish, little pond
    d. Big fish, big pond
    e. Other

2. How would you describe your life now and its place in the community?
    a. Big fish, little pond
    b. Little fish, big pond
    c. Little fish, little pond
    d. Big fish, big pond
    e. Other

3. When faced with the opposite of your "world" (you're used to a little pond, you like being in a big pond, etc.), what is

your reaction? Does it make you feel overwhelmed? Challenged? Inspired? Depressed? Other?

4. Add anything you would like to include about your parents and their roles in creating this world you grew up in.

YOUR PLACE IN THE FAMILY

Try focusing on your place within your family for this section. You can be as specific or as general as you'd like to be. Talking about our families paints a picture of who we are.

1. What was your birth order (oldest, middle, youngest, and number of how many)? And please note how many boys, girls, stepsiblings, etc.
2. Correlate your birth order to the stages of your life. At what point in your life did you feel the best? For example, if you were the baby of your family, would you say that your earlier life felt the most comfortable and successful for you? If you were the oldest, would you say the best is yet to come?
3. List each of your parents' birth order in their respective families growing up. Describe each parent's place and how they responded to the corresponding child. (For example, if your mom was the youngest girl, how did she feel about the youngest girl in your family, and so on.)

YOU AS A WORKER

Building on the previous theme from section 2, think about how you usually behave when you are in a group of people.

1. In what role do you feel most comfortable? (The wunderkind if you're the baby? The teacher/sage if you're the oldest?

The diplomat if you're in the middle? The center of attention if you're the only?)

2. Now define yourself as a worker. Do you tend to feel most comfortable at a job where your position correlates with your birth order?

3. Describe your parents in a group. To which parent are you most similar as a worker?

4. And just for fun, if this were *The Apprentice,* what role would you take? (Project manager? Worker bee? "Under the radar" type?) And at what point in the process do you think you'd hear "You're fired!"?

YOU IN A RELATIONSHIP
This section will help you observe your role within a relationship.

1. Think about the different types of people you've been attracted to throughout your life. Has there been one predominant type? Note their birth order as well.

2. Is there a personality trait you look for in a partner that "completes" you?

3. From what you've learned about your parents, do you usually take on the role one of them takes/took?

4. Recognizing that the world works on a yin/yang (feminine/masculine) balance, what percentage of each (within yourself) would you say *you* are?

YOU AND YOUR HEALTH/APPEARANCE/BODY
Now we're going to be talking about . . . *you* and your health/appearance/body!

1. What was your mom's attitude about her own health/appearance/body? What was hers about your father's?

2. What was your father's attitude about his own health/ appearance/body? His attitude about your mom's?

3. What were your mom's and dad's attitudes over the years about your health/appearance/body?

4. Compare your current health/appearance/body to that of your siblings.

5. Taking in all the information that you've revealed about yourself in the past five sections, what would you say you've learned about the way you currently handle your health/ appearance/body? Is there anything you'd like to do to improve it? And is there anything you've learned that will help you do just that?

Handwritten Diary Versus Writing on a Computer

Before you get too deep into your diary, decide in which medium you want to work: Should your diary be handwritten or typed on your computer? Students in my memory classes often claim that handwritten notations are easier to remember than those typed on a computer, because seeing your thoughts and ideas written in your own handwriting creates a stronger connection to the material. Despite the fact that typing is faster and details can better be captured before they fade, anything handwritten feels more like it's *yours*. Play around with what works best for you, which may be a combination of the two.

I learned a great deal about handwriting something to make it your own from working with Danny DeVito on *Taxi*. Throughout the day, he used to write out every one of his lines on bits of paper. When I asked him why he did this, he explained that by writing them out in his own handwriting, the lines became a part of him and a part of his character, Louie De Palma, at the same time. It was a way of bringing the two of them together as one. The conscious act of writing by hand made the lines change from being words written in a script by the talented *Taxi* writers—led by the brilliant James L. Brooks—to being words that Louie now owned.

My first husband, Frederic Forrest, used a similar technique as an actor. As he was learning a script, he wrote it out entirely by hand, printing his own lines and writing out the rest of the text in cursive. Writing in longhand also feels more organic to another friend, the legendary playwright Neil Simon. He uses a yellow legal pad and a Le Pen to bring his characters to life. In an interview in *The Paris Review,* he explained, "Sometimes I write on both sides of the page, but I always leave myself lots of room to make notes and cross things out . . . It seems to me that every script comes out of a computer looking like it was written by the same person."

These three great artists consciously choose to write out their material in longhand, in order to a find a deeper and more organic connection to their work. To someone who doesn't write or act, writing out the words to which you most want to feel connected may sound a bit eccentric, but it makes a lot of sense. When you are first writing or working on a character, you tend to do it in a conscious way. And that's why creating a role is much like living a conscious life.

Actually, if you ever wrote down notes in school, you already know this trick. Writing those notes helped you remember the material, because it required a mindful effort to make each notation. You could almost throw away the notes afterward, because most of them were already in your head.

A computer diary is obviously faster to use than a handwritten one, but it's not as easy to carry around with you to record moments of unexpected inspiration. The biggest advantage to putting your thoughts in a computer document is that it can be password protected, so you can express feelings without fear of someone else reading it. In many cases, that privacy is essential for many of the issues on your plate. You certainly don't want your partner to find your personal thoughts, such as suppressed anger and resentment, before you're ready to share them. Everyone needs and deserves privacy, and you need to have full confidence in what you are disclosing; otherwise your true feelings will be compromised. If you are in any way fearful of someone else reading what you're expressing, your entries won't be honest, and nothing will be accomplished. Honesty matters most. (In the diaries I've kept over the years I've written some entries in code, but even with my memory I've had to flash back awhile to remember the code!) Another possibility is to do a combination of both a handwritten (for easy mobility) and a computer-typed (for privacy protection) diary. I recommend keeping your diary moving forward on your computer (for speed) and filling it in as you go along, but if you *really* want to make something stick, write it out. The very act of writing will put it directly through to your brain and make it more a part of you.

Diary Alternatives

Along with the decision to write your diary by hand or by keyboard, there are some other options to consider. You may dread the thought of journaling, whether it's handwritten or typed, but there are alternatives. The idea is still the same, but because we are all different, and we have the resources and tools to take advantage of those differences, why not proceed in a way that's most appealing for your particular style? Similar to having different dominant senses, people also have their favorite ways of logging personal information. There is no right way to do it. Just choose what feels right to you! One example might be an audio diary. If you are the kind of person who doesn't like to bother with physically writing in a diary or typing on a computer, try using an electronic audio recording device (iPhone, BlackBerry, or pocket digital voice recorder) to input information. Within the last three or four years nearly every one of these devices has seriously expanded its audio storage capacity. Most can now store thousands of hours of recording time, which can easily be downloaded onto your computer for even more storage space. In many ways this is more efficient than using a handwritten diary/ journal. The words can just flow out of your mouth, with less temptation to edit.

Now you can almost record your entire life! But don't do that. You'll need an additional lifetime just to listen to it. So, unless you're Shirley MacLaine, narrow it down to what's important. The biggest downside to an audio-recorded diary is that accessing specific entries within your vast recording is not as easy as it is in a pocket diary or Word document. Transcription might be necessary once the information is captured.

But what good would understanding your past be if you weren't able to carry this newfound information into your present and then allow it to inform your future? One of the greatest advantages to developing a better autobiographical memory is that it opens your eyes not only to your past, but to the road ahead as well.

Up to now everything has been *retro*spective, bringing the past up to the present. Now you'll shift gears to become *pro*spective, bringing the present into the future and planning for memories in advance.

Part Three

RECOLLECTION

Maintenance and Enhancement

Chapter Eight

From Here on In

Moving Forward and Memory Maintenance

$\mathcal{I}$t was fun to go back and put the puzzle pieces of your past together and create a timeline and diary. Now it will be much easier, and highly beneficial, to document your life in real time, as you are living it, from this moment on. Your life from this day forward should have more awareness, significance, and integrity. You should be able to lead a more conscious and conscientious life, based on your many newly discovered connections from your past. Now that you've got a well-developed timeline of your life and have analyzed your life patterns—strengths, weaknesses, and most common triggers and pitfalls—you can design a workable course for your future.

After you feel satisfied with what you've excavated and analyzed from your timeline, you now need daily maintenance to stay on task and remain proactive. I suggest at least five minutes at the end of each day to record your thoughts: what you learned, your feelings, struggles, victories, and your plans for the next day—APR maintenance. That alone will be a tremendous help for remembering what is most important in your life, the lessons of each day, and the meaning in what you're doing. Do this before going to bed each night. It will become a catalogue of your most important moments, combined with what you've already documented in your diary. Just like the feelings elicited by your timeline, don't edit or stress out about your daily thoughts; just use two or three sentences or a few bullet points to record and define each day.

Maintenance Alternatives

Let me offer some suggestions on how to manage your memory maintenance. First, you can jot a few sentences down in your diary for five or ten minutes at the end of each day. This applies whether your diary is on hard copy or hard drive. If you created your diary on an audio recording device, I assume you will do the same with your diary maintenance. For the rest of these maintenance options, let's step outside the box and get a little creative.

Photo Maintenance

If sight is your strongest sense, you may want to document your life with images. Consider keeping a small digital camera with you at all times to capture the images that are most important through-out your day. Choose the moments that mean something and that you'll want to remember. If you are a visual person, this format will speak to you the loudest . . . or rather, shine brightest! This is so easy to do now that most mobile devices have cameras and you can take or delete as many photos as you like. I take pictures on my iPhone all the time now, and because I relate to my life in a very chronological way anyway, it's easy to find any picture when needed. You can annotate them as you like, or just reflect on them as you're waiting somewhere. Imagine how much fun it will be to look back at the end of the year at the thousand or so photos that tell the story of your year. You can even supplement your photos with short audio recordings. In the past, we would only consider this kind of daily documentation while on vacation, but now it's so easy to do this every day, because of all the wonderful electronic devices at our disposal. Why not treat every day like a vacation?

Shorthand Maintenance

For those of you who love to condense, consolidate, and cut to the chase, consider the following shorthand diary strategy. In order to recognize patterns by getting a baseline on what you're doing, you will use a simplified code to see patterns at a glance. But that may not tell the whole story, so you may need to add a line or two for clarification next to your code. I've kept many lifestyle diaries using shorthand like this over the years. It's great for condensing lots of information and saving time for every new entry. Here's how my shorthand diet diary worked. If, for example, I experienced a day with very little sleep (S), didn't exercise (E), ate too much food (F), and drank alcohol (A), my shorthand code for that day would be all bold, **S, F, A, E,** which normally would be a bad day. I put negative behavior in bold because I wanted that to stand out the most, since that was the behavior I was trying to change. Now, the code doesn't always tell the whole story, and an extra explanation entry is often needed for clarification. If next to this notation I wrote, "Went to a great party," there is an exceptional reason for breaking so many rules. I had a great time, so it was worth it to some degree. Now let's suppose your log for that day was **S, F, A, E,** and the explanation line was "Stayed at home and watched TV all day—too stressed to do anything positive." That tells a very different story, which is why an explanation line is necessary.

The code log shows certain patterns at a glance, especially when you're looking at an entire month or year. Think of the explanation lines as footnotes. Of course, you can use any code you want for this. Your code, however, should be designed based on what your priorities are for that year or the near future, as mine were for health and diet. As you look at the entire year or season using shorthand code, you may be saying things like, "Wow, I didn't realize I have been doing this since last June." Or "I see that I'm slipping back into my old patterns again. I was struggling with this five years ago, and I guess I haven't quite conquered it yet."

Instead of focusing on diet and fitness, your shorthand diary could be aimed toward your emotional health. Let's say a major emotional trigger you listed is anger—a big fat bold "A." (The last example listed "A" for alcohol, but your code will change according to your priorities.) Why not track the number of A events per week (road rage, snapping at kids or spouse, fuming at work, dumping on friends), see that it's an unreasonable number, then decide that you don't want to live life angry and decide how you're going to address it? Or perhaps you haven't been able to express your honest feelings to a family member, friend, or coworker, so you have been "eating" your anger by tossing and turning all night, not exercising, drinking, overeating, or taking it out on other people.

You're always trying to figure out what is at the root. Shorthand maintenance with initials can help you see patterns more quickly than when this part of your diary is written out in longer paragraphs, so be sure to add the initials to sum it all up regardless of how you first log it.

APR Calendar: For Daily/Weekly/Monthly/Annual Reviews

Now, if you want your daily diary maintenance to be more in-depth than two or three lines, a few photos, or shorthand code, this is it. An APR calendar/diary, designed especially for this purpose, will prepare you for the future, guide you in the present, and help you analyze what you've done in the past.

Because you now know the most useful way to use your APR journal, you will be actively analyzing your life as you're living it. Remembering what you did in your past is only part of your strategy. What good is documenting and remembering your life if it doesn't take you purposefully in the direction you want to go? You need to keep an APR calendar that is designed not just for documenting what you've done; it must also guide you to where you want to go.

Most diaries are designed for you to write down what you did each day *after* you did it, while most calendars, appointment books, or daily planners are designed to organize your *future* schedule. I want you to combine both kinds of tools into one APR calendar, while also focusing on the present. Here, you will be utilizing all the elements and benefits of autobiographical memory that we've discussed.

You can make your own APR calendar, or if you prefer, you can buy my Total Memory Makeover calendar (with APR notation and memory tips!) designed specifically for this purpose at the following website: browntrout.com.

If making your own APR calendar, each page should be given its own day, divided in three sections, like this:

Sunday, August 14, 2012

ANTICIPATION

_____
_____
_____
_____
_____
_____
_____

PARTICIPATION

_____
_____
_____
_____
_____
_____
_____

RECOLLECTION

_____
_____
_____
_____
_____
_____
_____

In the anticipation section, write down anything about that day before it takes place, whether it's months, weeks, or just the night before. Write down anything you are planning for that day: events, appointments, to-do lists, thoughts, anxieties, and whatever else comes to mind beforehand that has anything to do with that day. Use that section in the same way that you would use an appointment book, but also be sure to add any feelings you anticipate for that day.

In the participation section, write down anything that actually happened that day. Treat this section like an abbreviated version of a typical diary. The best time to write in this section is at the end of the day you're writing about or the next morning. Actually, the next morning is best, because your brain has had a chance to process the previous day's information and also recharge for better clarity. If you don't have time to write in the morning, try to do it sometime in that following day, while it's still relatively fresh in your mind. To save time and space, you can highlight anything scheduled in the anticipation section that actually occurred, rather than write it again in the participation section.

The recollection section should be used two days later to write down your analysis of that day—your feelings, observations, and anything else that comes to your mind when you refer back to that day. Feel free to use your own personal shorthand to save space.

Along with a page for each day, your APR calendar should also contain one page devoted to the start of each week, three pages devoted to the start of each month, and nine pages devoted to the start of each year, with each of those sections split into "Anticipation," "Participation," and "Recollection" subdivisions.

Let me give you some examples. Before your January 1 page, you will start with a nine-page section for the year (2013), followed by a three-page section for the month (January) and one page for the week (January 1–January 7). The first three pages of the section for the year should be labeled "Anticipation." This gives you space to broadly write down all your plans and goals for the year ahead. Use this section to focus your priorities, fix things that need to be fixed, build on projects already started, and, in general, move your life in the direction you want it to go.

Following those nine pages are the three pages devoted to the month of January, like this: 2013 January

<table>
<tr><td>

2013 January

ANTICIPATION

_____
_____
_____
_____
_____
_____

</td><td>

2013 January

PARTICIPATION

_____
_____
_____
_____
_____
_____

</td></tr>
</table>

2013 January

RECOLLECTION

_____
_____
_____
_____
_____
_____

Following that will be the one page for the first week of January.

2013 Jan. 1–7

ANTICIPATION

_____

_____

_____

_____

_____

_____

_____

PARTICIPATION

_____

_____

_____

_____

_____

_____

RECOLLECTION

_____

_____

_____

_____

_____

_____

_____

After the page for week one, begin the individual pages for each of the next seven days, until you get to the one page for the second week, and so on. This may seem a little complicated, but it's very simple when you see it laid out.

To help you see your year clearly, it's important to divide your information in this fashion. You'll be able to track exactly how long some tasks took to complete, which directions your path took at different times of the year, and how successful you were at accomplishing what you planned.

There may be times when you won't be sure where on the calendar to place certain information. Keep these rules in mind: Anything you're writing before the moment, day, week, month, or year goes in the anticipation section. Anything in the present or immediately following the present goes in the participation section, and anything that is entered more than a day after the moment has passed is entered in the recollection section. When deciding whether to enter information in the respective week, month, or day, consider how specific the information is. Anything that addresses your main priorities for the year goes in the APR section for the year. You only have nine pages for the entire year, so be selective. Anything that is more specific to a particular day or week goes in that day or week's section. Anything specific to your goals for the month goes in the three pages for that month, and so on. Don't be overly concerned about this process—you'll find your own personal way of inputting information that works best for you and your objectives. The calendar and its divisions by APR of days, weeks, months, and year will help organize your year for easier understanding and recall.

Maintenance Recap

Whether you keep an APR calendar, hand or audio journal, or photo chronology, your life will naturally take a more proactive, meaningful direction. You will quickly notice not only greater awareness of yourself and everything around you, but also *how* you are living your life. Keeping an APR calendar or any maintenance journal is like having a therapist in your pocket. You will be living and guiding your life at the same time. There will be no more randomness in your direction, and that change alone makes a huge difference in what becomes of your life. It's the difference between a boat that has a rudder and one that doesn't.

Designing Your Personal Constitution

When we review our lives in full, we see all the changes we'll want to make. Awareness is half the battle. I'm always explaining to my readers and students in my online lifestyle classes that if they really want to get healthy, they have to know what it is they're doing every day that may be thwarting their best intentions. You are now aware of your past mistakes and hopefully getting to the bottom of what has caused them. You are also learning to avoid mistakes in the future, because of the daily entries you are documenting in whatever form of maintenance diary you're keeping. We now have one more layer to add to your Total Memory Makeover arsenal.

Everything we've done up to this point has been about looking back and analyzing, observing yourself in the present, or envisioning expectations for the future. By now, you should have a really good sense of how you operate in a multitude of circumstances, challenges, and everyday moments. You know what you normally do in situation A and how you'll respond to this particular person in situation B. You also know that you feel great whenever you are about to embark on challenge C, and so on. When countries or companies are formed, a set of rules is created so that the country or company has something to refer to when decisions need to be made or disagreements need to be resolved. In the United States, we have our Constitution. It is the law of our land; it is our number one source for determining right and wrong and direction in our society. It has been altered and interpreted in different ways over the years, based on our country's changing needs and course. A constitution is important because it helps guide people with very diverse views to find common ground. A constitution is designed to resolve issues before they happen. Even though people rarely draft a personal constitution for themselves, doing so can be life-changing. It has the potential to provide unexpected breakthroughs for finding guidance and direction in one's life.

The process of psychotherapy begins with an early information-gathering period, in which you tell the therapist about your past, your intimate personal history, and how you got to the point you're at right now. This is necessary for the process, and it can take months or even years. Eventually, a point is reached where the therapist has gathered enough information to accelerate the therapeutic process. You are now at that point. The difference here is that *you* will be your own therapist. Think of your personal constitution as creating your own little imaginary guidance counselor who will always be with you, helping you make important decisions throughout your day. It's like having an angel on your shoulder, but he looks more like Sigmund Freud. You have already taken a good hard look at your past. You now know what you need most, how you operate, and where you are most likely to fail. For example, in the past when you've planned to lose weight, quit smoking, or stand up for yourself at work, you might have failed because these kinds of challenges are often approached in the same way we approach New Year's res-olutions. We say, "Starting at midnight, I'm never going to smoke or drink or overeat or whatever again." There's very little focus on *why* we failed in the past, like the (at least) thirty-three reasons for self-sabotage (anger, bad timing, boredom, carelessness, cockiness, control issues, depression, envy, exhaustion, fear of failure, fear of sexuality, fear of success, frustration, guilt, impatience, intimida-tion, jealousy, lack of commitment, lack of confidence, lack of prep-aration, lack of resilience, lack of self-importance, lack of willpower, laziness, loneliness, neglect, overcompensation, self-centeredness, self-deception, self-destruction, shame, starvation, stress, and so on!).

We approach these kinds of resolutions with amnesia. At this point, however, there should be no amnesia. You have almost your entire life laid out in front of you—what you've done in the past and what you hope to do in the future. You are in the ideal position, with the best perspective for designing a constitution for your future.

It is essential that a personal constitution be created with a calm, level, and objective mind-set. Don't decide how you are going to deal with your ex-husband right after you've had an argument with him. You must be emotionally removed from each item that will be addressed in your constitution. Find a time in your day that is not influenced by caffeine, wine, anger, fatigue, depression, or euphoria. I know, it's not often easy to find a moment like that that is so unfettered, but be patient. You'll find it. When you do, here's how you should proceed:

Gather everything you've created so far in this book—your time-line, your Track, your journal, and the results from all the exercises we've done. As you look through these, make a list of the things you most want to address in your life. I'll give you two examples to help you understand what I mean. One will be for John Doe and the other for Jane Doe.

FOR JOHN DOE

1. I spend too much time ruminating and complaining about rude, loud, and inconsiderate people.
2. I am not handling everyday stress very well and need to develop a better stress-management technique or attitude.
3. I rarely stick to my exercise program for more than a few weeks at a time, and I need to analyze why I continue the same pattern.
4. I shouldn't be eating heavy meats and salting my food, considering my cholesterol and blood pressure are very high.
5. I need to develop better time-management strategies, because I can't keep up with my workload and still have time for family.

FOR JANE DOE

1. I have been needlessly spinning my wheels with my ex-husband for several years now, with almost no progress or agreement on how to co-parent our daughter.
2. I need to move forward with my career by standing up for myself more at work.
3. I have been dreaming about a trip to Europe/Africa/Asia for over twenty years now. It's time to make that dream a reality.
4. I allow my fears to stop me from doing many of the things I love to do. I need to learn ways to relieve these fears and see things more rationally.
5. I tend to spend money needlessly when I'm depressed

and need a pick-me-up. I want to become more aware of
vulnerable moments like this and stop wasting money.

After you have compiled your "things to change" list, it's time to
begin writing your personal constitution. There are so many things
to consider as you analyze what you want to change. Change is difficult. It almost always requires some discomfort at first, even when
it is change for the better. If change were easy, you would have done
it already. You have to really think about what will be your obstacles
and pitfalls when making each change. Are you sure you even *want*
each change? Or have you gotten so comfortable with your situation that it's easier (or more fun) to complain than to take on the
responsibility of action? As you look at each item on your change
list, refer to your timeline and your Track for clues about why you
do the things you do and what you could do now that would be
different. Think about how your APR influenced each of these moments and experiences. How do you usually anticipate a meeting
with your boss, mother, or ex-spouse? Does the meeting (the participation phase) usually turn out the way you anticipated? How do
you usually feel afterward, during the recollection phase? Do you
feel good about yourself? Disappointed? Ashamed? It's important to
carefully break it down like this, in order to develop a concrete plan
of action for your personal constitution. You may seriously want to
lose weight, for example, and be very successful, at first. However,
those pounds will come back if you don't have a well-designed plan
from the beginning. But if you decide that you're going to see your
life through the prism of health, so that all your decisions are based
on being healthy rather than just weight loss, you have a much better chance of making your changes stick.

This is exactly what happened to me. After my father died, I
found myself "eating my feelings" and gaining a lot of weight. I yo-yo
dieted for years, sometimes swinging my weight twenty pounds in a

week. When my mom died and I realized I had to change my life, it was enough of a wake-up call to say, "This is not about my body; this is about my health!" I got healthy, dropped fifty-four pounds, lowered my cholesterol over a hundred points, and never went back to my former unhealthy habits.

Revisiting the list on page 169, and using Jane Doe again as an example, note the first item on her list: "I have been needlessly spinning my wheels with my ex-husband for several years now, with almost no progress or agreement on how to co-parent our daughter."

How should Jane proceed here if she really wants to change, or at least come to terms with this conflict? As Jane looks over her timeline and Track and uses all five of her senses in order to fully bring back those moments, she clearly sees that this has been an issue for almost ten years now. Most entries from her timeline involving her ex remind her of some kind of conflict, battle, or manipulation. She has been dealing with this for so long now, it's become a part of her routine. Jane needs to look carefully at each encounter to see if and when the outcome was more favorable than other times. Did she do anything different on those occasions, or was her ex just randomly in a good mood or doing something nice to manipulate her for something in the future? Jane needs to understand that she cannot change her ex-husband's behavior or perspective, especially since she hasn't been able to so far. She only has the power to control and change herself. It is very difficult to face the realization that some things can't be changed. People will spend years (sometimes decades) beating the same dead issue. We are creatures of habit. We get into ruts and have bouts of depression at certain times of the year, or even during brief moments in our day. Our standards get lowered, and we often respond with a knee-jerk reaction, rather than in ways that are rational and wise. Jane needs to understand how she usually responds when her buttons are pushed, especially when she's tired, depressed, or vulnerable, and she needs to find new ways to react that will guide the course of events in the direction she wants it to go. That is why it's important to create your personal constitution when you are at a levelheaded moment of clarity. That's when you will see your circumstances objectively. You will see new ways to respond and new ways to change what you want changed. When you do, write these down for each item on your list. These solutions for each of the items on your list will become your personal constitution.

Back to our example using Jane's item one, here's what Jane's solution might look like: "I have to be the grown-up and take the high road in each encounter with my ex-husband. I must stay strong and not get sucked into petty battles, as I usually do. I know this will appear as if I'm walking away or quitting at first. That's okay. He can think whatever he wants, as long as we avoid the confrontations that usually lead to an impasse."

Remember that each item you write about in your constitution is not written in stone. Changes and amendments will undoubtedly be required, depending on how well your new strategies are working. This is an ongoing process, and you will be tracking your life more carefully now with your APR calendar. You will now have all the resources to analyze your progress available at your fingertips: your timeline, your Track, a greater awareness, being in the moment with fully engaged senses, and an up-to-date APR calendar.

Chapter Nine

You Are Your Own Memory Palace

*P*oets claim that we recapture for a moment the self that we were long ago when we enter some house or garden in which we used to live in our youth. But these are most hazardous pilgrimages, which end as often in disappointment as in success. It is in ourselves that we should rather seek to find those fixed places, contemporaneous with different years.

—Marcel Proust

*T*o enhance the quality, frequency, and quantity of your autobiographical memories using all the concepts and tools in your memory toolbox—including APR; your Track; your timeline; and Horizontal, Vertical, Mushroom, and Sporadic remembering—it's time to use your own life to remember!

Autobiographical State of Mind

Along with your outline, timeline, and journal, there are other ways to exercise your autobiographical memory. One is to periodically put yourself in an autobiographical state of mind. The perfect time to do this is when you're sitting in a waiting room, stuck in traffic, or trying to fall asleep at night. Decide that you're going to hunker down for a bit and give yourself over to remembering something. This can take anywhere from a minute to ten minutes, or as long as you'd like to reflect on a particular memory. I still do this all the time, and that's not to say that I am always purposely time-traveling with my memory and not thinking of the future or the tasks at hand. Ruminating on the past can definitely be a meditative and therapeutic alternative to stressing out about the present (considering that 90 percent of what we worry about never happens, anyway!). You can revisit the situations that seem similar to those about which you are currently deliberating, because it helps settle your emotions and connects the dots of what was similar to your present circumstances. There are many ways to do this, and most of the exercises in the book thus far can be repeated and expanded now that you are more in the practice of taking yourself back to a memory. And they can be a lot of fun, once you get the hang of it. Any of the sense-memory exercises from chapter 3 can be reproduced using different objects connected to your timeline/diary, of course, but now it's time to try your version of the time-traveling I did when I was on *The Early Show*.

EXERCISE #16: TIMELINE TIME-TRAVEL

Picture your personal timeline of a particular year in your head (this year, last year, or any special year in your past).

- Now try to fill in as much of it as possible.
- Start with a wide viewpoint and then try to narrow your focus to what you did on your birthday, your kids' birthdays, anniversaries, holidays, vacations, or siblings' birthdays.

- Add another layer to this exercise by taking the memory from a simple meta-tag into deep recall—from Horizontal to Vertical, or Mushroom or Sporadic.

At first, this may seem very challenging, but the more you do it, the more you'll enjoy exploring in this way. Always start with a wide scope and continually narrow your focus. You could also start with a year, then a season, then a month, then a week, then a day. Don't be surprised if you can eventually narrow it down to the hour or even a minute.

> *Before I met Marilu, my memories were a jumbled mess. I would hop from one thing to the next . . . a sort of mental-imagery ADD. After spending time around Marilu and in her classes, I've learned to almost categorize my memories or only allow myself certain times to think about a string of memories of a particular person, place, or time. For instance, if I go on a long run, I'll plan what I'll allow myself to think about to help the time pass. When that particular mile is over or that time has passed, I will move on to something else. Sometimes I have to pull myself back from a tangent; however, I've definitely learned from her the beauty of seeing the memory through.*
>
> *Along the same lines, when I swim laps, I have created a way to make the laps helpful to my memory. Each lap is dedicated to a year of my life. It is amazing to me how I get out of that pool with such appreciation for a great workout and realize that I have had a really interesting life!*
>
> *Another thing I eventually learned from all of this is that I do not need to keep things to hold on to my memories. I'm going to remember certain events, regardless of whether or not I have a trinket, program, or photo from that event. If I don't*

*remember off of the top of my head, I can usually calculate
the day based on events surrounding the activity or particular
instance. It is a slow process, but there is a dramatic difference
in what I keep now vs. what I used to hold on to for fear I'd forget. If it is in my heart and/or my mind, it is there to stay!*

—*DeAnn Wehner (Marilu.com member)*

Memory Pegs and Memory Palaces

I am a firm believer in using what you already have, making a few
minor adjustments, and developing it into something even better.
Why start from scratch? This goes for everything, from putting together a wardrobe, to creating a diet plan, to decorating your home,
to developing memory strategies. Most people don't realize how
close they already are to what they are trying to accomplish, which
brings us to using your whole life to help prompt your memory.

A memory palace is a particular and familiar place, such as your
home, work, street, or school that is used in your mind to remember information. Memory pegs are images used within a memory
palace. Both are commonly recommended in memory books. They
often work very well, but they are limited.

One of the problems I have with memory pegs and palaces is
that they seem one step removed from what you are trying to accomplish. For example, to remember a grocery list, I have heard two
different strategies recommended. One suggests standing in the
center of your kitchen and working clockwise around the room connecting each item you're trying to remember with an object in the
kitchen. Using my kitchen as an example, I would look at my refrig-
erator and think orange juice, look at my toaster and think bread,
and so on. For the second method, I would imagine the orange juice

carton exploding in the fridge, and the bread in the toaster on fire (or some other cartoonlike image). And I would continue this for each grocery item as I connect it to each object in my kitchen.

This would never work for me, and maybe not for you either. When I want to make a grocery list, I use the grocery store itself. I already know the layout of my local Whole Foods, so I just imagine walking through the store to make my list. This works very well for me, because it cuts out the middleman. My kitchen is not where I shop, so why would I want to create a false structure when I can use the exact location where I'll be shopping? I can imagine myself right in Whole Foods and see where the food is actually shelved in the supermarket. I don't need outrageous images; I just need to be conscious of the store while I am there. This feels much more connected than being once or twice removed, never mind that you're going to have to come up with different images unless you plan on getting the same old groceries each time.

When remembering your life, instead of using something outside of it like a memory palace, I recommend going right to the source itself. Whatever you need to remember, why not use the real deal? All the places where you've lived and worked and played really exist or existed. You don't have to imagine or use unrelated structures to stage your memories. You can put each memory right where it took place.

Your life itself is your own unique memory palace, which contains an accumulation of everything you've ever experienced. The things you find while sifting through your attic and basement were an actual part of your life. They are not inside an imaginary house that you empty and then fill up again to reuse for more memories, or on a temporary slate that you keep wiping clean so that you can reuse it. This is a location with an unlimited capacity that you continue to fill. You can go deeper and deeper, as you continue to find out more information about your past and then build on that. It is cumulative, because it continues to build as you uncover moments and memories that you thought were lost. Your brain is the ultimate memory palace!

Thinking in Numbers

I was married to Marilu for eleven years. We have two beautiful, brilliant sons. One year, we found ourselves in Rome, Italy, and we wanted to go to the world-famous restaurant Sabatini. I called down to the hotel concierge and got the number, and knowing Marilu's faculty, it was easier just to repeat it to her than to write it down. (By this time, a habit.) She fed it back to me, and I dialed the number and made the reservation. So far, nothing really to write home about.

Four years later, we were back in Rome and decided we would like to have another one of those great Sabatini meals. I just picked up the phone, but this time, instead of calling the concierge, I asked Marilu for the number, and she rattled it off like it was on the tip of her tongue. I called, and we shared another marvelous meal.

I have always recognized her amazing memory, but one of the things that stood out to me at that time was that Italian phone numbers aren't like ours; they have no exchange to break up the pattern. They are just eight random numbers in a row that she could store away with millions of other strings of numbers, faces, colors, and incidents that she always has current and available to reference anytime in an instant.

In all the time I've known her and in her entire life, and I believe it's true to this very day, Marilu has never had a personal phone book on her phone, on her computer, or recorded in any other way but in her mind. In fact, I have never even seen her write down a telephone number. And I've known her for over twenty-seven years.

—*Rob Lieberman*

Numbers are everywhere! Each day hundreds, if not thousands, of combinations of numbers cross our paths. All that is needed to remember numbers is to build a little on top of what's already there. When it comes to phone numbers, passport numbers, bank accounts, your social security number, or your driver's license number, it's easier than you think to commit them to memory. It's actually easy to remember dozens, even hundreds of account numbers in your head—as long as you develop some kind of system for storing them. There are numerous systems used for remembering numbers. Rather than learn a new one from scratch, try building on the one you are already using naturally. You may not be aware of it, but you're probably using some kind of system right now for this.

When I started doing my memory classes on Marilu.com, I was surprised how many people wished that they could remember numbers better. People would complain that they could remember the home phone number of their best friend from high school but had to check their cell's contacts to call their office for the hundredth time. I think this discrepancy might be a result of how people remember rather than what they can remember. When you're young, you don't think about how you're remembering things or wishing you could remember more. You're simply repeating a string of numbers enough times that it gets stuck in your head, and because this is one of the first numbers you've had to remember, there is plenty of clean space. You're young and undistracted, but this only lasts so long. As we get older, our minds aren't so clear and focused on what we're doing. We need more than we did before to remember a string of seven numbers—a strategy or a technique.

EXERCISE #17: WHAT'S YOUR DIGITS?

In keeping with the "you are your own memory palace" idea of this chapter, I suggest you remember numbers by relating them to your life. I have inserted a chart of every possible two-digit combination here and I want you to go through and find all the numbers you have an obvious memory for. For example, "52" reminds me of my birth year and "46" reminds me of April 6, my birthday. I can go through this chart and associate every one of these numbers with something from my life. Now when you have a phone number to remember, break it into two-, three-, or four-digit pieces, and it'll be much easier. You'll be connecting ideas from your own life rather than abstract or absurd notions. Besides, the more you start relating your life to dates, the more dates and experiences you'll have to draw from.

For example, I have a friend whose phone number's last four digits are 4780. The first time I heard this number, I instantly thought *April 7, 1980! It was a Monday and I went to Francis Ford Coppola's birthday party!* And I flash on this event for a second whenever I call my friend. But this is not unusual for me because *every* time I hear *any* number, I relate it to some date from my life. (I promised you'd get to see how my brain works!) I even help other people think of ways to remember their numbers. Why rely only on your cell phone's contact list? We have to stop being so lazy and start using our brain's amazing abilities!

NUMBER CHART 00–99

00	01	02	03	04	05	06	07	08	09
10	11	12	13	14	15	16	17	18	19
20	21	22	23	24	25	26	27	28	29
30	31	32	33	34	35	36	37	38	39
40	41	42	43	44	45	46	47	48	49
50	51	52	53	54	55	56	57	58	59
60	61	62	63	64	65	66	67	68	69
70	71	72	73	74	75	76	77	78	79
80	81	82	83	84	85	86	87	88	89
90	91	92	93	94	95	96	97	98	99

Cross-Referencing Your Memory with World Events

Of the many tests I was given at UC Irvine to determine whether or not I had HSAM—and there were over five hundred questions in one day—the one that has become the standard for determining HSAM is based on current events. I can't give you all the questions I was asked, of course. But I can tell you that cross-referencing your autobiographical memory against what was happening in the news on a particular day is a surefire way to meta-tag your memories. The daily news offers information that is always available to you and everyone else.

For instance, as discussed previously in chapter 2, we all have a collective memory based on adrenaline-producing events like 9/11 and JFK's assassination. But what about less well-known events that you know for sure happened, you're just not sure when? Entering these current events on your diary/timeline will help ground your personal memories in a way that will make it easier to retrieve them, should you ever forget where you put them in the first place.

A perfect example of this came up recently when I was explaining to an interviewer my role as a consultant on the new CBS show *Unforgettable*. It's about a female cop with HSAM named Carrie Wells (and played by the fabulous Poppy Montgomery!). The producers had sent me the script for a particular episode in which Carrie is discussing a party she and another character attended on Saturday, July 17, 1999. I explained to the producers that if they wanted to keep that date in the script, someone with HSAM would immediately know, as I did, that there would be no way to talk about it without mentioning the fact that it was the same weekend that John F. Kennedy Jr.'s plane tragically went down in Martha's Vineyard. The accident got nonstop television coverage, and Carrie would definitely cross-reference her party reminiscence with this shattering world news event. I told the producers they should either address this in her dialogue or change the date of the party, which is what they ultimately chose to do. Every time I have told someone this story, I have first asked, "Do you know what Carrie would talk about on July 17, 1999?" Of the ten people I have asked, only one person knew at first mention. But as soon as I shared what happened that weekend, a flood of memories came back *for every single person*!

EXERCISE #18: WHERE WERE YOU WHEN . . .

In this exercise, look at this list of world events and try to remember where you were when you first heard or read about them. Even if you can't remember the exact time and place, see what other memories these events prompt in you. If you draw a complete blank, don't give up, just look up the dates or events and cross-connect them with your personal timeline to see what else you may remember.

1. The Oklahoma City bombing
2. The shootings at Columbine
3. The death of Osama bin Laden
4. The taking down of the Berlin Wall
5. The shooting of Ronald Reagan
6. Baby Jessica's rescue from the well
7. The *Challenger* explosion
8. The death of Michael Jackson
9. The election of President Obama
10. The rescue of the Chilean miners

Chapter Ten

It's All in the Family: Paying It Forward

In seeking wisdom, the first step is silence, the second listening, the third remembering, the fourth practicing, the fifth—teaching others.

—Solomon ibn Gabirol

One day when my boys were two and three and a half years old, I was giving them a bath and thought, *Here is a perfect opportunity to work on their memories.* How often were my normally very active kids going to be sitting there with nothing to do but get clean? I realized that the bath could be a place for not only exercises in hygiene but exercises in memory, as well. So I devised a game that would teach them something about their family history and get them thinking and recalling on a daily basis. I dubbed this game *Who, When They Were Little . . .*

As I was one of six siblings in a very tight-knit family, my kids have always been very close to all of their aunts and uncles. Naturally, they have been curious about what these relatives were all like when they were little kids. I have a very colorful family, and we were even more colorful as children. It was a wonderful environment to grow up in, and it lent itself to lots of great stories and facts. The six of us had very different personalities and tastes, especially when we were small, so my boys and I loved to play this game. Nicky and Joey would pick a category (for example, birthday cakes), and I would say, "Who, when they were little, liked coconut cake? Who, when they were little, liked chocolate cake?" and they would have to guess which of my siblings was the correct answer. Or I'd ask, "Who, when they were little, got hit by a car when he didn't look both ways while buying Mister Softee?" With every category, my boys would learn a lot about their relatives and about life, as well. My boys remember just as much about my brothers and sisters as children as they do about each other. And in fact, my siblings think my kids know more about them than *they* remember about each other!

I have always been the family historian, so I guess I have always felt a responsibility to keep these memories fresh. And why not? Memories are a family affair. Why not get the whole family involved in extending everyone's memories, across the generations? Everyone remembers something, and judging from what I've seen on Facebook, I know that all you need is one person to start an e-mail or thread about something your family has shared. In fact, while working on this book, Lorin and I decided to test this phenomenon. We initiated a family e-mail asking everyone to spark their memories about past family vacations and events. I purposely didn't start listing my memories, but waited until others got the ball rolling (lest they think I was just showing off!). Interestingly enough, it wasn't my siblings who couldn't wait to contribute to the challenge, but rather the next generation of kids (the Facebook users!) who dove right in and shared whatever memories they could about the past. I could see in black and white the value of those early memory games and exercises. Being able to pass down the family folklore not only builds your kids' memory fitness, it also boosts your parenting effectiveness when you're able to tell them relatable stories from your past. What kid doesn't love to know their parents have been through good and bad times and have gotten past them?

EXERCISE #19: MEMORY BRAINSTORMING FORUM

This exercise can really be fun and provide some unexpected memories from a long-lost past. While working on this book, Lorin posted on Facebook a few prompting questions about a crazy musical revue he did in Chicago back in 1977. He posted it for five former cast members he recently reconnected with on Facebook.

As each person responded, they naturally added a comment or two and shared a random memory from that experience. In just three days and about thirty posts later, this little forum snowballed into remembering and recounting highlights from every musical number in the show, the first and last names of all the other cast members, great little side stories Lorin had completely forgotten about, photos exchanged from the show, and a campaign to locate the rest of the cast. He got much more than he bargained for by posting a few remembrances from an oddball show he did thirty-four years ago. This is amazing, considering most of the cast members are now grandparents. This kind of thing happens every day on Facebook, which provides a perfect forum to do it.

Your exercise is this:

- Start a memory brainstorming forum with your family, friends, coworkers, classmates, former band members, sorority sisters, bridge club, or bowling team.
- All you need to do is post a question, song, photo, poem, theme, specific event, or anything else that will get the discussion ball rolling. If you're not on Facebook, you can still do it by creating a mass e-mail for your group.

This is really fun to do with older siblings, because everybody seems to have a different spin on the same event that happened decades ago. Whether it was a family vacation, holiday, or wedding, everyone remembers things a little differently. Anyway, give it a try. You have nothing to lose, and you might rekindle some old warm and fuzzy nostalgic feelings.

Teaching Others What You've Learned

Developing your autobiographical memory is the first step toward teaching your kids to develop a better memory and being a more effective parent. As adults, we often forget what it was like to be young. We may remember *having* the experience, but we don't remember *feeling* the experience, and certainly not from a child's point of view. By analyzing moments from your own childhood and teenage years, you'll be able to understand and relate to your kids in a more meaningful way. Greater focus on details from your past will bring out those feelings and help you provide better parental guidance. Rather than just sympathizing with your children's needs and feelings, you'll be able to empathize with them. This opens up communication so much more and allows you to really understand your kids, and sometimes for your kids to actually feel like you "get" them.

I experienced the parental memory benefit a few months ago when my husband, Michael, received a text message from his granddaughter (my step-granddaughter), Victoria, who was fourteen at the time. She and my son Joey are only six months—but one generation—apart, even though Michael and I are the same age. (He had his kids early and I had mine late!) Victoria was contacting her grandfather because she wanted to go with four of her friends to a "rave" on Melrose Avenue, in Los Angeles. According to my son Nick, "The raves in large cities like Los Angeles can be drug-ridden affairs where twentysomethings and misguided people younger than that can enjoy each other's sweat and apparent lack of self-awareness." Maybe safe, but probably not terribly smart, because you never know.

Victoria wanted to know if Michael could pick up her and her friends and then let the gang stay the night with us. As soon as I heard about these proposed arrangements, I knew we had to find out more about the event. It came to light quickly that there were going to be some problems. It wasn't long before we found out that the pickup time was five A.M.! In the morning! When rats are hitting the hay! *That* five A.M.! Here was a fourteen-year-old girl, and she wanted to be picked up at five in the morning, and my husband was considering it?! My immediate response was, "Are you kidding me? It's a *rave!*"

I told him, "Trust me, you and I are going to be worried about these kids long before midnight. This whole idea is pure mental guacamole. Victoria is in way over her head." The more I read her communications, the clearer it became that I was right and that she was really way too young for this whole thing. Reading her texts, like, "Thank you, thank you so much. This means so much to me, Papa!" I got the feeling she was trying to look cool to the older teens, as if to say, "Hey, my grandpa lives nearby, so he could pick us up, and he's really hip and won't question anything." And even though I was amused that anyone would think Michael is hip, I knew that this was not okay.

As this situation unfolded and we waited for more texts to come in, I had time to sit and think about where this situation made my mind travel. I was instantly taken back to one particular night when I was Victoria's age, a few months shy of my fifteenth birthday. It was Friday, February 24, 1967, and I was in rehearsals for *The Unsinkable Molly Brown,* a musical I was doing at my high school. Just like Victoria, I was frequently trying to fit in with older kids. Most of the other students in the play were juniors and seniors, but because I had a special dance in the show, I was the only freshman in the production. On this particular night, I was hanging around with some of the older girls, including one very mature eighteen-year-old. She and her twin sister shared their own apartment, which they had recently rented to get away from home. I admired them for being so emancipated and fun, like Janet Leigh and Betty Garrett in *My Sister Eileen*, but their independence was unusual, especially for 1967.

So on this Friday, after rehearsal, we went to a neighborhood Polish restaurant/bar. This group of kids often did this on non-school nights, and I would tag along to get a snack and hang out before my dad picked me up. While we sat in the restaurant, we heard one of our favorite songs on the jukebox coming from the adjoining bar, so we decided to go in and dance to it. I understand now why this made the local barflies so happy, but back then I was thrilled by the attention. We certainly didn't want to disappoint them after they enthusiastically clapped and cheered (all in Polish!) and then cleared some beer mugs for us to dance . . . on top of the bar— while still wearing our school uniforms! I imagine their thinking, *Nothing says "Thank God it's Piątek" like drinking an ice-cold pint of Żywiec while watching high school girls dance on the bar.* Now, you can picture how my father reacted when he got out of his car and walked down the street, only to see his fourteen-year-old daughter doing a scene from *Coyote Ugly* . . . Polsky style!

Victoria's situation brought me right back there, to that moment. The image of seeing my dad and the men in the bar, what my uniform looked like and felt like, the feeling of embarrassment when I realized just how naïve I was. I don't think I was in any serious danger that night, but it could easily have turned out that way. You're unaware of a lot when you're a teenager. You want to feel like a grown-up, but you don't really understand what that means yet. Teens often get themselves in sticky situations and can't always find their way out. They make decisions based on how they want to appear, rather than what seems safe or what is true to them. Elements of this scene kept flashing back to me the more I heard about Victoria's plans and her thinly veiled fears of being uncool and unsafe.

Yet Michael was still considering the idea. His indecision might have been a result of ignorance. I'm still not sure he even knows what a rave *is*. That night, my son Nick told Michael and me, "Raves attract the bad kids. You can be sure that some substances will be involved, and the kids there will not be the kind you'll want around Victoria, not to mention the fact that her 'friends' are the ones who want to go in the first place." Unfortunately, Michael was a true sailor in his youth, and he believes in the strength of his word. Michael had already agreed to take Victoria and felt he had to honor that agreement. But flashing back on my memory made me realize how important it was to intervene and keep this rave date from taking place—so I had to insist. He wrote back to tell Victoria that he wouldn't take her.

She wrote back a simple "Okay." Even though her response was full of disappointment, I definitely found out from our conversation a week later that she was relieved and very grateful we had saved her from herself. In her heart, I don't think she really wanted to go in the first place, and Michael's definitive no gave her a way out with her friends. She now had someone else to blame and didn't have to injure her reputation. She didn't have to say that her parents wouldn't let her, because only the logistics of getting a ride home were to blame. I know for a fact how much she liked that.

Strong memories allow us to understand the young among us better, because we can truly relate to what they're going through. Since my incident at the bar, I have never caved to peer pressure. How could I, when I remembered in such vivid detail the terrible feelings that accompany that weakness? Even as a child, I knew I wanted to make something of my life, and I sensed that a bad reputation could follow me forever.

I have continually reminded my children of this and later told Victoria the same story. She smiled when she heard it, because she realized that I, too, was once a young teenage girl who was in over her head, and she felt understood.

I have always tried to teach my sons to stand up to peer pressure and always be proud of being different. Nick has never had trouble standing up for himself.

Nick was less than four and a half years old and in pre-K at his new school when I received a call from the vice principal on Thursday, September 17, 1998. He told me that there had been an all-school assembly (students three through eighteen years old) to discuss the possible discontinuation of wearing school uniforms. As usual, the students sat on the gymnasium floor with the youngest kids in front, and the microphone for the students to make their comments was placed near the fourth-grade classes. This was because no child under that grade had ever addressed the school or had anything to contribute to the assemblies.

Until that day.

The vice principal was calling to tell me that Nicky had walked from his pre-K row back to the fourth-grade group, stood on a chair to reach the microphone, and shared his opinion with the entire school.

"I think we should keep wearing uniforms because what if someone doesn't have nice clothes like someone else? They might feel bad. But if we are all wearing the same uniform, we are all the same."

The school decided to uphold its uniform policy, which stands to this day.

Perhaps Nick's confidence comes from stories I've told during games like Who, When They Were Little . . . that contained a lesson. One such story I told them was a moment in college when I proudly stood up to peer pressure.

In 1970, at the University of Chicago, I was staying in what had just become U of C's first coed dorm. At the time, the dorm committee was trying to decide whether to make bathrooms gender-specific or coed (remember this was the hippie era!) and announced that this would be decided democratically, adding that the vote had to be unanimous in order for the bathrooms to be coed. Without hesitation, I interrupted whoever was running the meeting and said, "Let me save you the trouble. I don't want to share a bathroom with guys—period." I think a lot of the girls felt the same way; they didn't want to share with the boys either, but the fear of looking prudish in this very public setting controlled their actions. (Imagine what other peer pressuring would have gone on had the vote passed! Or don't.) Nevertheless, because I wasn't afraid to go against the tide, I ended up with the only non-coed girls' bathroom (out of four) right outside my dorm room.

Later, of course, girls from the other floors started using that bathroom, because they too were uncomfortable sharing theirs with guys.

Lessons like this are worth remembering, because they come back in different disguises throughout your life. Being able to draw from your past in detail allows you to recognize these same conditions, no matter what shape they're taking at the moment.

Perhaps Nick learned to stand up for himself from hearing stories like that.

Teaching Kids to Have Great Memories

Each day of our lives we make deposits in the memory banks of our children.

—*Charles R. Swindoll*

There is no doubt that memory exercises enhance whatever ability with which your children are born. You can't leave it all to genetics—memory must be developed, and the earlier you start, the better. Even though I took to heart my father's APR approach to life, I never had anyone work directly with me on my memory, but I frequently wonder how many people there would be with HSAM if more parents taught memory skills. You'd certainly have a lot fewer tennis pros if kids had to invent the game, and those of us with great memories basically had to invent our own techniques. We didn't have coaches, but instead we just stumbled into developing this skill. As previously stated, it's like a muscle in your body that needs to be exercised. And when you actually exercise it, your child's memory development and recall will exceed your expectations.

I believe it's never too early to plant seeds that will help kids learn something faster later. Because I have always wanted my children to have great memories, I've done memory exercises with them since before they started walking. I used lots of picture books and, especially, one children's picture dictionary. I would point to each picture and tell them what it was. "This is a cat, and she says 'meow.' This is a cup, and you sip it like this. This is a phone, and you talk into it like this." I would do dozens of these and then I would go back and say, "Which one is the cat? What does she do?

What do you do with a phone?" Months before they started talking, they would point to the right picture and make the sounds or do the action that fit with the picture. I also did this with family photo albums, where I would point to the pictures and tell stories about the various people. I wanted to get their memories stimulated from the beginning, and so I even included details I knew they wouldn't understand at the time. I hoped these details would give them a head start toward making that connection further down the road. Who, When They Were Little . . . was just one of many memory games we played.

I can remember the very first day I did a memory exercise with my son Nick, who was four months old at the time. It was Monday, September 19, 1994, and I was going off to work on my talk show, *Marilu*. Nicky was the kind of baby who was always comfortable with other people. He never cried when I left the house, but this particular morning, he was teething and a little sad, and I could see the tears welling up in his eyes as I walked toward the door. Realizing I would only be gone for a short time, I wanted him to know I'd be right back, but I could tell he wasn't understanding exactly what my words meant.

I then remembered the power of music. I have always known that the ABCs are memorable to kids because of the tune attached. I knew, too, that people with Alzheimer's often forget their spouse or their own name, but they will remember the lyrics to a song. I decided that whenever I wanted Nick to remember some communication, I would attach it to a melody. "I'll be right back!" was repeated to a particular tune. And when teaching him at eight months old to roll onto his stomach and then slide off a bed, "How do you get down?" was said to another tune. As soon as he heard these different statements sung to their respective tunes he knew *exactly* what they meant. He understood the tunes so well, in fact, that I didn't even need the words to convey the intention.

Over the years, for both of my boys, I connected tunes with many different communications, and I have to believe this helped strengthen their minds and memories. My son Nick was talking in sentences before he was one and reading fluently before he turned five. And Joey, who is eighteen months younger than Nick, talked and read early, as well—he also demonstrates signs of HSAM and will be tested when he is older. He and I love to challenge each other with dates, and sometimes I purposely give him the wrong day of the week just to keep him on his toes. But his memory is incredible. In fact, since he was two years old, there has never been an adult who could beat Joey at the classic game Memory, including me!

EXERCISE #20: INFANT MEMORY GAMES

It is never too early to start doing memory exercises with your baby. In fact, lots of studies show that babies respond more favorably (being calmer, crying less) to specific music that was frequently played out loud while they were . . . in the womb! So, feel free to crank up the Mozart or Carlos Santana, starting in the second or third trimester. Your baby will be playing Name That Sonata before he can even say "Da Da," and he'll be the life of the pre-K party, shaking groovy bossa nova rhythms on his teething rattle.

Along with music, visual identification games are also great.

- Use pictures from books, magazines, and family photos. Clearly describe what they're looking at, and then go back and ask them to point out the image you're naming or describing. At first, this may seem futile, but eventually you'll have what you might call a "Helen Keller wa-wa" moment, and they'll start accurately picking out everything.

EXERCISE #21: WHO, WHEN THEY WERE LITTLE . . .

When you play this game with your children, use members of your family or friends, or anyone you knew when they were young. Pick different categories, from favorite animals to favorite TV shows to birthday parties to crazy school stories—even to childhood injuries like breaking an arm and needing a cast. Even if you don't have all of these facts in your memory bank, you can ask your siblings or family members. They will certainly remember their own childhood preferences. Talk about a memory-stimulating conversation!

APR for Kids

As Nicky and Joey got older, I made up games that were a little more sophisticated. Just like my father did before me, I explained the three parts to every event—the anticipation, the participation, and the recollection. For example, on our way to my sister's house, I would say, "Okay, where are we going? Who will be there? What do you think we're going to do there?" Then on the way home, I would ask them, "Did we do the things you thought we would? What happened that was different? What were some of your favorite moments?" When we traveled around the country for eight months, while I was performing in the national company of *Annie Get Your Gun*, my boys and I would often use APR to discuss our future, present, and past experiences. I'd periodically ask my then–four-and-a-half-year-old and six-year-old things like, "What city are we in? What city were we just visiting? What was the name of the restaurant we ate at last week? Describe the park from that city where Daddy came to visit us." To this day, my boys can describe in detail our on-the-road experience in 2000 and 2001, and it was twenty-two cities in thirty weeks!

In large part because of these exercises, my kids became very good at predicting, observing, and remembering events. People are always surprised that my sons, now sixteen and seventeen, remember so many details from when they were quite young. The boys actually challenge each other's memories often. I hear them debating about when something was or how it happened. They test each other on the details of a person, place, event, or experience, and it can get very competitive and heated. I'll even throw out challenges to them. By doing this, I am helping them develop strong memories, while fine-tuning their five senses. It's sort of like Family *Jeopardy!* and I'm Alex Trebek.

I asked my older son if he thinks having a good memory has helped him in his life so far. He told me that being able to recall events and seeing my memory in action over the years has made him more present and conscious. Throughout this book, I have encouraged you to take in more information on a daily basis to improve your memory. My son was basically saying that he worked the other way; the conditioning of his memory has made him more aware and able to live more in the moment than he would be able to otherwise. That's the paradox and beauty of memory; it's a two-way process. The more you are present and able to take in information, the more you will be able to remember it later on.

I may be wrong, but I don't think people are very aware of their memory. They like when they remember something and they think about their actual memories, but few people concern themselves with the at times inscrutable and deeply layered process of memory. I have a mother who, for obvious reasons, thinks a lot about memory, and she was never shy about pok-

ing and prodding us to exercise our own. But of course as a child, I wasn't aware of my "parenting." I really did see all of these things as games, and to this day, my brother and I prefer games based around information rather than luck or even skill. And what is learning and schooling, especially quizzing and testing, other than one very long, multifaceted, information-based game? I try to balance a love of experience with a love of raw information, and I think my mom's influence with her games and questions has allowed me to think like that. Knowing your memory makes you aware of your mind. You have to imagine what it's like for good memory not to be seen as a party trick, but instead as an imperative, something that you can't live without. My mom's developmental memory games have probably given more mental direction to my life than anything else.

—Nick Lieberman

EXERCISE #22: THE MEMORY GAME

Play your own version of the Memory Game with your family. Just like Who, When They Were Little . . . , the Memory Game can be about anything you do.

- From your family vacations to different holidays to birthday parties, different school years, and different teachers, use any experience that your children have had, even as simple as one day at school.
- Create questions based on your family's experiences with any of these categories and tailor them for each participant. That way, even the younger family members can get involved.

- Be sure to periodically re-ask the questions to keep the memories alive. Many years after the fact, my kids can answer questions like, "In what city did we visit the Rock and Roll Hall of Fame when you guys were five and six?" Or "What did each of your Secret Santas give you for Christmas in 2002?"

Memory is, by definition, the exploration of what is stored in our minds. It is relating one thing to many things or many things to one thing, forming interrelated networks of experiences and lessons. And the best thing about the Memory Game is that it can be played anywhere, anytime, and can have a level of competition that's genuinely fun.

Chapter Eleven

Memory and Health

I couldn't write a book about memory, or any book for that matter, without talking about the importance of good health. It is often said that when a physician or dentist looks at a person's teeth, gums, and tongue, it's like a mechanic looking under the hood of your car. Both give you a fairly good first impression of a person's (or car's) overall health. Imagine how well we could define a person's health or psyche if we could scan and get a printout of his or her memory. If the conditions under a car's hood were analogous to dental health, then studying a person's memory would be analogous to putting your car through an intensive computer diagnostic analysis. Every single detail (past, present, and future) about that person's health would be revealed, because our brains, our memory, and our overall physical and mental health are so profoundly connected. If you've read any of my *Total Health Makeover* books you know that health is about much more than what you eat. Memory and health go hand in hand; it's not possible to have one without the other. Diet is, of course, vitally important to our well-being, but there are many lifestyle choices that also affect your memory. Being smart and making the right choices in these areas can have an enormously positive impact on your overall cognitive function. In this chapter, I will give you the basics for good memory health, starting with what I consider to be the number one key to living a healthy lifestyle.

Learn to Love the Food That Loves You

I talk about healthy lifestyle choices in my *Total Health Makeover* books, in my public appearances, and on my website, and this has become my credo. Our bodies are designed to eat what nature intended, yet most of us eat what factories manufactured. When you eat right, your body responds with a big thank-you. Eating what nature intended (fruits, vegetables, legumes, and whole grains) may sound a little boring to most people, but that perception usually comes from a junk-food-polluted palate. Years of eating junk food (heavy meats, dairy, white flours and sugar, cakes, and overly processed, chemicalized fast foods) can drastically change your perception (palate sensitivity) both physically and mentally. Eating a junk-food diet naturally leads to *craving* a junk-food diet. Unfortunately the brainwashing began when we were too young to remember or do anything about it. The American diet *is* a junk-food diet, and, of course, that is what nearly all of us were raised on. Thankfully, this perception can be changed. Someone who claims not to like green vegetables has probably had a limited exposure to that category. He can't possibly have tasted every green vegetable there is or experimented with the many different ways to prepare them. (You wouldn't write off an entire state because you didn't enjoy your layover at their airport!) The same thing applies to foods sampled only one way. Don't limit your dietary choices. As an adult you have the ability to treat yourself to broader horizons. Open yourself up to the adventure of trying hundreds of fresh foods you've barely glanced at in the produce department. It is possible to learn to love the food that loves you, but it takes a spirit of adventure, a little discipline, a little experimentation and effort, and a certain amount of commitment. Trust me. The payoff is tremendous. You will have more energy, better digestion, and a stronger body. Your breath, your moods, and your enjoyment of food will all change for the better, too. When treated and fed properly, your body chooses vibrancy, energy, and healing. Food from nature is the greatest of all medicines. As Hippocrates said, "Let your food be your medicine and your medicine be your food."

Your mental function and attitude has the ability to change a great deal when you switch to a healthier lifestyle, and your brain is the most important component of all this. Choose foods that are best for your brain, because they happen to be best for everything else, too: high-antioxidant fruits, hearty colorful root vegetables and dark green leafy vegetables, whole grains, and heart-healthy proteins such as beans and fish. This is a "tip of the iceberg" list. Each one of these categories can have literally dozens of entries.

In addition to choosing "brain food," cut down on alcohol and caffeine and boost your fresh water intake. Water is restorative and cleansing. It gets everything moving, including your thoughts. Many times when you think you're hungry, you're probably only thirsty. So, the next time your mind feels stuck, grab a glass and water your brain!

Try to be inventive as you prepare your brain-healthy food. Creating new recipes exercises your brain, and when you do this with friends and family, it becomes both a cognitive and social activity. This is "healthy" multitasking: getting in the kitchen, enjoying the color, the taste, the friendship, and the process of creating meals together. It's not about what you "have to" do. It's about what you "get to" do. You get to connect with others, which is a healthy brain activity itself. Doing this with a partner can be very sensual. When you're in a steamy kitchen with the love of your life, slicing into juicy fruits, tasting sauces, you've got all sorts of opportunities to heat things up. The healthiest activities really are the most fun.

There's no downside to experimenting and trying new food. You get to be creative and immediately enjoy the results of your creativity. Talk about instant gratification! Taking the time to step away when you're moving at a hectic pace is good for your body and mind. And, as if all that weren't enough, you're also creating memories. Use your APR calendar and jot down some of your plans for trying new foods and recipes. How great is it that *creating* memories can help you strengthen your memory? Once again it proves that "Everything is connected to *everything!*"

Memory and Diet

Diet is a key component of healthy brain function. *Everything* functions better when you are eating healthier. Here are some brain foods and tips you should know about.

Get Back to Nature

Natural foods don't contain artificial sweeteners, additives, or colors, but are rich in antioxidants, vitamins, and minerals. Avocados, brown rice, walnuts, brussels sprouts, legumes, oatmeal, fish, almonds, pumpkins, oranges, soybeans, spinach, barley, carrots, cantaloupe, beets, and berries are just a few examples of natural foods. If your plate is colorful and most of what you're eating looks pretty much the way it does in nature, you're doing well.

I talk a lot in my other books and on my website, Marilu.com, about eating whole foods. The best foods for your body are the ones that haven't been messed with to improve appearance, enhance flavor, or increase shelf life. If natural foods aren't currently a big part of your diet, start introducing them. If there was something that you hated eating as a kid, something that you always left on your plate, you probably don't want to start with that, although sometimes we surprise ourselves years later when we retry something we hated in childhood. Just keep an open mind and a willingness to taste with a new perspective. If you still hate it, that's okay. There are hundreds of other foods for you to try. Find a grocery store with a great produce department, or visit a farmer's market and just have fun looking at the things that aren't familiar to you. One of the best things about fruits and vegetables is the fact that they aren't packaged, so you can buy a small amount and see if you like it.

Over time you'll cleanse your palate and want more and more of these live, health-giving foods. There's nothing like the taste and texture of *real* food. Everything is there: color, flavor, crunch, creaminess, tartness, and sweetness. It's all there in nature. Organic food is becoming more available. As it becomes more mainstream, the prices are coming down in some areas. Check out local farms and farm stands. A package of frozen veggies doesn't have the same nutrients or vibrancy as the same vegetable picked only a few hours earlier.

Eat the Rainbow

Antioxidants help protect your brain cells and keep mental functioning at a high level. Fruits, especially citrus fruits, and many vegetables are antioxidant rich. Eat more oranges, bananas, apples, raspberries, strawberries, tomatoes, mangoes, kiwis, and blueberries. If the vegetables you're most familiar with are French fries and iceberg lettuce, then it's time to add color to your plate and try some red beets; orange carrots; green broccoli and spinach; and red, yellow, orange, and green peppers. You get the picture—in living color! In order to balance free radicals in the body it is important to eat foods rich in antioxidants since these help reduce the damage of oxidative stress in the brain. As we age the natural antioxidants produced by our body tend to decrease, and this increases the risk for more memory-related problems, diseases, and age-related issues.

As an added bonus many of these colorful foods require little or no preparation. Fresh fruits are delicious and refreshing, and many contain a high water content, the importance of which we already discussed. Wet foods are like getting extra bonus points when it comes to staying hydrated. Some of the crisper veggies, such as carrots and beets, are especially good roasted. Peel and chop and toss them in the oven with a little olive oil and sea salt. Soon your house will fill with amazing aromas followed by a gorgeous meal on your table.

Getting the antioxidants into your diet is so easy . . . and you can make it fun!

Take in More Fiber; Take Out the Trash

Fiber is an integral part of food digestion and helps make sure your brain gets the nutrients it needs. With the proper amount of fiber in your diet your brain works faster and is able to focus better. Fiber helps increase brainpower, mood, memory, and attention by providing the brain with the nutrients that start antioxidant action. This process helps to prevent dementia, Alzheimer's, and overall degeneration of the brain. Studies have shown that cognitive performance was improved in people with high-fiber diets that were low in sugar and refined flour. The fiber stays in your body's system longer but without the fast rise in blood sugar that you get from foods with refined sugars. If you incorporate the fruits, vegetables, and grains we've been talking about into your diet, you'll be well on your way to following this tip and getting the fiber your body needs to stay healthy. Everyone who ever had a grandmother has been told that fiber will help keep you regular. Constipation is unhealthy and leads to disease, which negatively impacts your ability to function.

Whole grains are a good source of fiber, so remember to apply the same principles you do for exercise and vegetables—don't judge all grains according to the instant cereals you had as a child. There are so many options out there and endless ways to include them in your diet. We've all seen barley as a soup ingredient, but it can be a great breakfast food, healthy and satisfying, especially in winter. You can also use it as a salad ingredient in summer with cranberries, onions, and parsley or as part of a post-workout snack on top of a salad that includes lean protein and legumes. If you're already familiar with quinoa you know that it's got a high protein content compared to other grains. It's also great in salads, in veggie burgers, or as a breakfast cereal with a little cinnamon and rice milk.

You Are What You Eat!

It should go without saying that if you eat poorly then your body will be in bad shape. This is also true in regard to the brain, obviously. Eating fatty, high-sodium junk food will cause a lack of energy, poor concentration, and other health problems, including the most serious illnesses, heart and cardiovascular disease, liver failure, stroke, and diabetes. I'm not talking about olive oil, nuts, or fat from fish (omega-3). These are all healthy fats. I'm talking about food that you'd find at a fast-food restaurant: processed meats, fried food, bacon, chicken skins, and so on. Think of the foods that have fat added and nutrition subtracted. Those are the foods to avoid.

There are good fats and there are bad fats. If it's being handed to you out of a drive-through window there's a good chance it's a bad fat. Studies suggest that fatty foods have an immediate impact on short-term memory and cognitive function. It is believed that high-fat diets impair the proper use of glucose in brain function. In an article titled "Fatty Foods Cause Memory Loss in Diabetics: Antioxidants the Solution?" Daniel H. Rasolt states that "unhealthy foods . . . cause more free radicals in the body, which can damage brain tissue," and that this increase in free radicals occurs as quickly as three hours after a meal high in fat or sugar. Look carefully at your overall diet. If most of the fat you consume is coming from natural whole foods, then you're doing well. Everyone has a story about a grandfather who ate a high-fat diet and lived a long vital life. But Grandpa never shouted his food choices into a plastic cartoon character and had dinner handed to him in a greasy sack. According to a study by the *New England Journal for Medicine*, "For the first time in two centuries, the current generation of children in America may have shorter life expectancies than their parents." Breakthroughs in medicine can no longer outperform the American fast-food diet, which is amazing considering medical break-throughs are coming faster than ever due to the recent exponential growth of information technology. How much are you a part of this trend? Be honest and take inventory of how many of your meals are coming out of a fryer. You can take control of that starting today.

We all lead busy lives. It's a different, faster-paced world than it was even twenty years ago, but planning ahead and employing some of the tools in this book can make it easier for you to arrange healthy meals for even the busiest day. Using a little APR in planning ahead and enjoying your healthy meal will ensure your recollection won't be that of an upset stomach!

Get Real!

There is a lot of evidence to suggest that any ingredient with the word "artificial" next to it is very harmful for your brain and body. These substances offer no vitamins, no nutrients, and no minerals! Stay away from the following: artificial food colorings and flavor-ings, artificial sweeteners like aspartame and acesulfame K, soda and other high-sugar drinks, hydrogenated fats, and any white flour products. Anything artificial accumulates in the body and over time causes memory loss and health problems. Think about this: Artificial colorings added to our children's drinks are *banned* in some countries! Also, the preservative sodium benzoate, which is used in many of our foods and beverages to extend shelf life and prevent spoilage, is also used in cosmetic products and automotive parts to prevent corrosion. Did you know that some cherry flavorings are also used in rubber dyes and plastics? There are some pineapple flavorings that are also used to clean textiles and leather. We are getting to a point where there is little difference between the products on the shelves *above* our kitchen sink and the ones *below*.

Do you really want to be eating food that could double as floor polish or deodorant? Food additives destroy important neural connections between healthy brain cells. These items are more merchandise than they are food. The more processing involved in a product, the more likely that product will contain chemicals and additives. Some of the more common problems associated with the three thousand additives in use today include tumors and serious side effects in lab animals; heart, lung, and kidney disease; birth defects; nausea and vomiting; and dangerous levels of toxicity and carcinogens. If you think the amount you ingest is minuscule, consider this: The average American consumes over a pound of food additives a year. Kick them to the curb and make room for the more delicious life-giving foods.

Give Up the Kiddie Cocaine

Avoid things like candy, processed cakes, processed cereals, and anything with white sugar since these are highly processed carbohydrates. A lot of people think of sugar as a neutral ingredient. They know it doesn't yield any benefits but they also don't believe it causes any harm. They couldn't be more wrong. Sugar is *not* an innocent ingredient. I've often referred to sugar as kiddy cocaine because of the way it stimulates mood swings and can be addictive, especially in children.

But these negative effects aren't just kid stuff. They also occur in adults. There are many studies that point to sugar's connection with hyperactivity, mood swings, digestion problems, and—for the purpose of this discussion—decreased brain activity. Sugar affects the parasympathetic nervous system, which is responsible for keeping the body in a state of balance and aiding recuperation after experiencing pain or stress. The circulatory and lymphatic systems can become invaded and the balance and quality of the red corpuscles change.

Sugar contains little or no nutrients, so sugary foods can cause the body and brain to eat away at its own storage of vitamins, minerals, and enzymes. If you eat refined sugars in abundance you actually risk poisoning your bloodstream with something called carbonic poisoning. Carbonic poisoning is the result of an accumulation of waste throughout the brain and nervous system, which increases brain cell death. The waste comes from the body's being unable to properly metabolize the refined sugars you've put into your system. The increase in those sugars forces the body to deplete its storage of minerals in trying to metabolize the sugar. From here the waste enters and "clogs" the bloodstream, causing symptoms of carbonic poisoning. An article in *Psychology Today* revealed a link between consumption of refined or processed sugars and an increased risk of depression and schizophrenia. The article states, "Refined sugars impair some of the naturally-occurring hormones in our brains; one of these hormones affected by refined sugar (specifically BDNF) has been shown to play a crucial role in memory, neuron functioning and growth." They also note that people diagnosed with depression and schizophrenia have "critically low" levels of the hormone BDNF. This is pretty serious stuff. Would you want to put yourself at risk for the sake of bleached white bread or cellophane-wrapped chocolate cupcakes? They don't call 'em Ding Dongs for nothing. Eliminating refined sugar doesn't mean that you'll never enjoy bread or dessert again. It means that you'll enjoy better bread, made with whole grains, and better desserts made with healthier sweeteners such as molasses and agave. After you change your palate to appreciate and crave nature's sweetness, you will be turned off to processed, artificially sweetened flavors. It's not about deprivation. It's about replacing inferior foods with those of higher quality.

On Your Mark, Get Set . . .

After a full night's sleep your brain is in need of replenishment. Having breakfast refuels your brain by supplying the energy and proper nutrition it needs. Several studies done on children, adults, and seniors published in the *American Journal of Clinical Nutrition* show improved memory as the result of having breakfast. A nutritious breakfast has been shown to improve learning ability, promote faster and clearer thinking, improve attention span, increase problem-solving ability, and improve overall emotional and mental health. Your brain functions by using glucose (a simple sugar and carbohydrate that your body uses as an energy source) for fuel. In fact, 90 percent of the brain's energy comes from glucose carried to the brain through the bloodstream. During the hours that you are sleeping, your body starts to run out of glucose and is forced to use stored fat, which is a less efficient fuel source. Breakfast is important because it bumps up your glucose levels and maintains a healthy body and brain. Eating a healthy breakfast is like throwing some small twigs on a fire to get those mental flames rising again. If you toss a log on the embers you're going to kill the fire. In the same way, a healthy breakfast (I recommend beginning with cleansing fruit) will stoke your metabolism and prevent you from feeling famished later in the day, forcing you to toss a big old log on the fire when you pig out at lunch. As we talked about earlier, you want this meal to be of good quality. Don't reach for the sugary cereals or a bagel from the drive-through. With a little advance planning you can have a healthy, whole-foods breakfast ready in minutes. That's going to give you a better start to your day and help you to be more productive. It's the foundation, the cornerstone, for the rest of your day.

Keep Alcohol Consumption Under Control

There's a Hindu proverb that says, "Even nectar is poison if taken to excess." It is known that alcohol kills brain cells, and if consumed in abundance (more than twenty-one drinks per week for men, or more than fourteen drinks per week for women) it can destroy your brain, body, and memory. According to the National Institute on Alcohol Abuse and Alcoholism, evidence of impairments to the brain, such as difficulty walking, blurred vision, slurred speech, slowed reaction times, and weakened memory, can be seen after only a drink or two. Women are considered more vulnerable to the health effects of alcohol then men. Alcoholic women develop more health problems after fewer years of heavy drinking than men. Men and women with severe drinking problems can develop two brain-damaging diseases: thiamine deficiency and Wernicke-Korsakoff syndrome. Thiamine deficiency, or lack of vitamin B_1, is the result of overall poor nutrition due to alcoholism. Vitamin B_1 is an essential nutrient for proper brain function, and over 80 percent of alcoholics have this deficiency. Wernicke-Korsakoff syndrome is actually two separate syndromes: Wernicke and Korsakoff. Wernicke syndrome causes confusion, paralysis of eye nerves, and problems with muscle coordination. Korsakoff syndrome causes severe and constant learning and memory complications. Alcohol also interferes with the body's absorption of vitamin B, zinc, potassium, and iron—all-important nutrients that affect proper brain function.

The next time you're having drinks, try these healthy rules of thumb: No more than two at a time. No more than five a week. Two glasses of water for every alcoholic beverage consumed. It will keep you hydrated and help mitigate the effects of the alcohol. You'll have the glass as something to hold and the water will prevent you from consuming too many drinks. Yes, you'll still be fun at parties *and* you'll remember everything that went on. You'll want to think about *what* you're ordering as well. One light beer is not the same as a creamy, sweet blender drink. Do you really need all the sugar and calories in that glass?

Remember other points we covered in this chapter and think about putting down your glass and seeking out someone whose conversation will make the night memorable. You could make a business connection, or a personal connection, that could be very important in your life. Why miss out?

Move It or Lose It

We all know that person who seems (and looks) older than they are. Chances are they're living a very sedentary (or destructive) lifestyle. Conversely we know people who are active well into their senior years. At a certain age they start to be described as "sharp as a tack" because people expect the elderly to be less acute, but would you want to match wits with Mel Brooks or Maya Angelou? What about Jimmy Carter or Alan Greenspan? Twyla Tharp is still working and looking wonderful at seventy. Paul Taylor is also active in the dance world at eighty-one. And would you dare to suggest that Clint Eastwood is past his prime? (It's important to note that Clint also maintains a fabulously healthy diet!) What do these people have in common? They have always been physically active and emotionally engaged.

Physical activity is *vital* because it increases blood flow and oxygen to the brain, as well as the rest of your body. The Department of Health and Human Services recommends at least a hundred and fifty minutes of moderate aerobic exercise a week, such as brisk walking or light jogging. Alternatively, you can do seventy-five minutes of vigorous aerobic activity, such as jogging or aerobic dancing, spread throughout the week. Research reported in the *Proceedings of the National Academy of Sciences* also concluded that aerobic exercise not only improves but also prevents shrinkage in the hippocampus, our memory center. A one-year study of seniors over sixty divided into two groups (toners versus aerobic exercisers) found that the anterior hippocampus actually *shrank*, on average, more than 1 percent for the toners, versus an average *gain* of 2 percent for aerobic exercisers.

What does this mean to you now? Get out and play. What's your favorite sport? Find something that you love and find a way to *participate* without a remote. You don't have to play competitively but you can find a league, or find your old racket and hit a ball against the concrete. When Lance Armstrong was recovering from cancer surgery he got on his bike. On one of his first rides, he was passed by a middle-aged woman out for a recreational ride. He just kept moving, and we all know where that ride led him.

Just find the activity that you enjoy most and then get out there and *have fun* with it! Sign up for classes that meet every week. You'll feel good and make new friends. Just make sure that activity involves plenty of oxygen. Don't just do weights to sculpt your body; you've got to do lots of sweating and breathing. (I know what you're thinking, and *yes*—go for it! That's another one of those multitasking activities. Good for your health, helps you connect with someone you love, and if you're lucky, it can be *very* memorable!)

I sometimes refer to exercise as the missing ingredient when people are pursuing a healthy lifestyle. Getting oxygen to the brain is a no-brainer. Getting out of the office for an hour of exercise can make you that much more effective when you get back to work.

People who think they don't like exercise are a lot like people who think they don't like vegetables. You can't possibly have tried every kind of movement there is. Don't like running? Try dancing.

Don't like dancing? Try a rebounder. Think of the scene in *Big* when Tom Hanks and Elizabeth Perkins are jumping on the trampoline. The kid in you wants to jump and play. Adults call it exercise and suck all the fun out of it. Tap into that mind-set you had when you wanted to stay out and play "just five more minutes." What activity will make you want those extra minutes?

Brain-Booster Supplements

There has been a lot of talk lately about the benefits of brain-booster supplements such as omega-3 fatty acids, folic acid, ginkgo biloba, co-enzyme Q10, and DHA, to name a few. If you take *any* supplements, always read the label carefully first for potential side effects and other warnings and consult your physician. So far it seems these supplements are safe and studies have shown them to significantly improve brain and memory function. Students are using them to rev up their study sessions and improve test scores, seniors use them to stay sharp and improve mood swings, and even patients suffering brain trauma such as strokes are showing noticeable improvement from them. It may be worth trying them to see if they do what they claim to do, but proceed with caution. Take less than the recommended dosage at first, and pay close attention to any side effects you may experience.

Medications and Memory

Prescription medications used to boost or restore brain function are usually much more potent and dangerous than supplements. Most are used to treat Alzheimer's patients and others suffering from memory loss. The most common drugs in this category are designed to increase levels of acetylcholine, which is a major neurotransmitter in the autonomic nervous system. It is also the only neurotransmitter used in the motor division of the somatic nervous system, which is responsible for relaying messages from the brain to the muscles. Drugs acting on the acetylcholine system are either agonists to the receptors, which work to stimulate the system, or antagonists, which work to inhibit the system. Drugs designed for memory loss and Alzheimer's patients are agonists, so they stimulate the system. Typical side effects are pronounced gastrointestinal difficulties and liver damage. More than 50 percent of patients prescribed acetylcholine stimulators are unable to reach the full dosage because of side effects. These medications *do* work, but at what cost? All prescription drugs come with great risks! Be aware when watching any pharmaceutical commercials on TV. Pharmaceutical companies are required by law to verbally reveal all the potential side effects of the drug, but that doesn't stop them from distracting the audience at the same time with the most visually stimulating moment of the commercial. As the voice-over announcer is rapidly mentioning diarrhea, blurred vision, anal leakage, and bad breath, a skater is doing a triple axel, the Viagra couple is doing a sexy tango dip, or the guy with the enlarged prostate is catching a home-run ball at Yankee Stadium. Think about it. They've got a lot to hide. When it comes to pharmaceuticals, I always think of the old adage "Show me a drug without side effects, and I'll show you a drug that doesn't work."

There are other drugs and vaccines that are still in the experimental stage for treating memory loss. Some sound promising for potentially slowing the progression of Alzheimer's disease, but we need to wait for more data. In the meantime, do your best to stay healthy, active, natural, and happy.

Use Your Brain!

Staying mentally active is a lot like exercise. If it's a part of what you enjoy, it's something you'll want to do. Planning parties, organizing activities, being the family historian, working crossword puzzles, reading sections in the newspaper that you usually skip, doing Sudoku puzzles, driving on alternate routes, or playing brain games with your kids are all wonderful activities. Don't think of these as "exercises." Always keep them fun. These are games, so think of them as playtime. If you like board games or charades then that's what you should be playing. Throw occasional game-night parties for your friends or do it every week with your kids. (When they were younger, my kids looked forward to every Friday because that meant game night!) A study at the Mayo Clinic concluded that these kinds of activities minimize the risks for developing memory problems, especially for people over age fifty. In the study, participants included a group who were already diagnosed with mild cognitive impairment. That group showed the most improvement when they engaged in puzzles, games, computer activities, reading, and crafts. If you have an older relative, try getting involved with them in this way. Share books, play games, or do puzzles together. In fact, you can do this as a volunteer at any nursing home, as well. You'll sharpen your own mental acuity while doing something nice for others. Think of what you can gain from a conversation with someone who is a generation ahead. When it comes to memory, everyone has something to offer. You can often find a mentor in an unlikely place.

Lastly, intelligent conversation can be one of the best tools for keeping your mind sharp. Eleanor Roosevelt is credited with saying, "Great minds discuss ideas; average minds discuss events; small minds discuss people." Chances are you know someone in each category. Invest in relationships with someone in the first category.

Party Hearty

Make it a priority to get together with friends and family. In the same extensive study mentioned above, the Mayo Clinic also discovered that just plain interacting with other people helps ward off depression and stress, which are two big contributors to memory loss. People who were socially active on a regular basis cut their memory impairment risk by 40 percent. A study published in the *American Journal of Public Health* also concluded that strong social interactions help preserve our brain health as we age. A key factor for cognitive decline in the elderly stems from social isolation. This is a very sad fact.

People are naturally drawn to others. We are social animals and need to interact with people daily. Even those who aren't naturally outgoing need to have some ongoing relationships and interaction for their emotional well-being. Introspection is wonderful but you also need to get out, interact with others, and take in new stimuli to stay happy and sharp. This applies to people of all ages. You don't have to be a senior to benefit significantly from frequent social interaction.

Don't limit yourself to your existing social circle. Maybe some of the tips in this chapter will have you trying some new activities and meeting new people. The unfamiliar can really help you refocus your objectives and inspire you to bring your A-game. You'll discover new friends and probably learn something new about yourself.

Setting Up Your Environment to Win

Health is a total picture, so why make things difficult for yourself by cluttering up your living or work space with so much junk that your mind can't process new information or remember anything because it's too busy sorting out the chaos? Set up your environment in a way that makes it easy to find what you need. Designate specific spots for important items that often get misplaced: keys, wallet, pens, scissors, glasses, cell phone, gym pass. Things go missing because they are not always placed in the same location. What items do you tend to lose? Where should each of them be? What makes it easiest for you to grab your keys and go? Where are you when you most often need your glasses? Give every item a home and then discipline yourself enough to place it there each time you use it. The repetition will become second nature and burned into your memory after a while. People ask me all the time if I ever lose anything or forget where I put something. I have assigned most things a site and tend to put them back in place. (Most of the time, anyway!) And the times I panic and say, "Where are my glasses [or keys, or wallet]?" I just have to stop and retrace my steps in my head to remember where they are. Believe it or not, as I was writing this, Michael couldn't track down his keys, and Nick couldn't find his book. I made Nick think back to where he last read his book and reminded Michael what happened after we got home last night, and they both found their lost items. I'm sure most people already retrace their steps naturally, but if your things have been consigned to a location, you won't have to do it as often. When you organize a business, everything needs to be arranged so that production is most efficient. If you think of your life and your memory as a business, you have to organize your environment so that it functions at full capacity. Clutter and bad organization contribute to stress; stress contributes to the dysfunction of everything, including memory. By organizing your belongings and schedule, you're stacking the odds in your favor. You're setting up your environment to win.

Chapter Twelve

Final Thoughts

While wracking my brain trying to figure out what final message I wanted to leave with you, my husband Michael said, "Maybe it's better to have someone who doesn't have your memory explain what it's like for one of us to have learned some of the lessons in this book? Besides, you've already asked siblings, best friends, and ex-husbands to contribute. Let me write something."

He was right. So here it is.

After knowing each other in college, Marilu and I finally got together in 2003. To say that you can remember all of your birthdays when you are eighteen is one thing, but at fifty, it is another thing altogether. Marilu had absorbed a lifetime of memories in that fantastic life she had led. Through it all, her memory continued to soak up, to organize, to make available all of the memories from all of the days—all of the sunsets, all of the Sunday afternoons, all of the workdays, the holidays, and even the boring, nothing days.

I have spent countless mornings lying in bed with Marilu and going over all of our Christmases together, our birthdays, all of her sister's birthdays, all of the August 28ths of her life. This is fun for

Marilu. It is exercise and it is recreation, and it comes with a great gift—the ability to revisit your past at any time, to enjoy it, to learn from it, be amused by it, or just pass the time in it. I understand now what I did not understand for many years. Without the validation of memory researchers like Dr. McGaugh, I might never have truly understood Marilu's gift. And I might never have appreciated what she has taught me and how it has changed my life.

I can go deeper into long lost memories because I have lived with Marilu these past nine years, and I have picked up some of the techniques she talks about in this book. I am now able to let myself go into a memory, and I can feel it and taste it and sense it. I can examine my past with more anticipation of what I will find and remember than with the dread of what I might dredge up and want to forget. I know that if I recollect events from the recent past, the memories will stay more current and fresh in my mind. I will live with the glow of a good time for a longer period of time. And if I live more of my life with gusto, and go for the Juice in everything I do, my memories will be that much stronger.

Having known Marilu from a long time ago, I knew about her memory and originally thought, that's great, but so what? After being with her for the past nine years, however, I now realize that just as this memory of hers defines who she is, so too, do all of our memories define who we are. Many people ask me what it is like to be married to a woman with whom you can never win an argument. I always say that in my case I am just the guy who knows for certain he will not win an argument with his wife, and so does not bother to try. The truth is that remembering my past has been the best therapy for me, and it has enriched my life immeasurably. Without Marilu and her insights I may not have overcome the many challenges of my life, sickness, the loss of parents, the stress of business. By being able to tap into my past I have indeed taken charge of my future.

I hope you now feel the same way.

Bibliography

Adams, William Lee. "The Truth About Photographic Memory." *Psychology Today* 1 Mar. 2006.

American Music Therapy Association. "About AMTA." American Music Therapy Association, 2009. 18 May 2011. <http://www.musictherapy.org/>.

Belluck, Pam. "Another Potential Benefit of Cutting Calories: Better Memory." *New York Times,* 27 Jan 2009.

Belluck, Pam. "Children's Life Expectancy Being Cut Short by Obesity." *New York Times,* 17 Mar. 2005. Web. <http://www.nytimes.com/2005/03/17/health/17obese.html>.

Black, Rosemary. "Autobiographical Memory: When You Can Remember Every Last Detail of Every Day of Your Life." *NY Daily News,* 21 Dec. 2010.

"Brain Food—The Types Of Diet To Feed For Optimal Mental Functioning." *GeniusIntelligence.com: Increase IQ And Intelligence. Become A Genius At Last!* 13 May 2011 <http://www.geniusintelligence.com/brainfood.htm>.

Britt, Robert Roy. "Scientists Study How Music Stirs Memories." *Science on MSNBC.com.* Live Science, 26 May 2005. <http://www.msnbc.msn.com/id/7995265/ns/technology_and_sciencEscience/t/scientists-study-how-music-stirs-memories/>.

Capozza, K. L. "Scientists Find Clues To Memory Health." *Earth News, Earth Science, Energy Technology, Environment News.* United Press International, 12 July 2005. <http://www.terradaily.com/news/human-05v.html>.

Cooney, Elizabeth. "Can Music Help Alzheimer's Patients Build Memories?" *The Boston Globe,* 17 May 2010. <http://www.boston.com/news/health/articles/2010/05/17/music_adds_memories_for_alzheimers_patients_more_protein_means_fewer_broken_hips/>.

Draaisma, D., Arnold Pomerans, and Erica Pomerans. *Why Life Speeds up as You Get Older: How Memory Shapes Our Past.* Cambridge: Cambridge UP, 2006.

Erickson, Kirk I., et al. "Exercise Training Increases Size of Hippocampus and Improves." *Proceedings of the National Academy of Sciences.* 31 Jan. 2011. Spring 2011 <http://www.pnas.org/content/early/2011/01/25/1015950108>.

Ertel, Karen A., ScD, M. Maria Glymour, and Lisa F. Berkman, PhD. "Effects of Social Integration of Preserving Memory Function in a Nationally Representative US Elderly Population." *American Journal of Public Health* 98 (2008): 1215–1220. <http://ajph.aphapublications.org/action/showMultiple Abstracts>.

Exforsys Inc. *Memory Skills.* 20 July 2006. Exforsys Inc. <http://www.exforsys .com/career-center/memory-skills/photographic-memory.html>.

Foer, Joshua. "Kaavya Syndrome." *Slate,* 27 Apr. 2006.

Foer, Joshua. *Moonwalking with Einstein: the Art and Science of Remembering Everything.* New York: Penguin, 2011.

Friedman, Richard M.D. "Traversing the Mystery of Memory." Ed. Abraham Ph.D. Kuperberg. *Behavior Health Digest* 9.4.

Henner, Marilu, and Lorin Henner. *Wear Your Life Well: Use What You Have to Get What You Want.* New York: HarperCollins, 2008.

Higbee, Kenneth L. *Your Memory: How It Works and How to Improve It.* New York: Prentice Hall, 1988.

Hsu, Jeremy. "Music-Memory Connection Found in Brain." *Current News on Space, Animals, Technology, Health, Environment, Culture and History | LiveScience.* Live Science, 29 Feb. 2009. <http://www.livescience .com/5327-music-memory-connection-brain.html>.

Hunter, Beatrice Trum. *The Sugar Trap and How to Avoid It.* Boston: Houghton Mifflin, 1982.

Ilardi, Stephen Ph.D. "Dietary Sugar and Mental Illness: A Surprising Link | Psychology Today." *Psychology Today: Health, Help, Happiness.* The Depression Cure Blog, 23 July 2009. <http://www.psychologytoday.com/blog/the -depression-cure/200907/dietary-sugar-and-mental-illness-surprising-link>.

Janata, Petr, S. T. Tomic, and S. K. Rakowski. "Characterization of Music-Evoked Autobiographical Memories." Center for Mind and Brain, University of California–Davis, *Memory* 158(8), 845–60 (Nov. 2007) <http://www .ncbi.nlm.nih.gov/pubmed/17965981>.

Johnson, Glen. *Traumatic Brain Injury Survival Guide.* Traverse City, MI: G. Johnson, 1998.

Johnson, Julene K, PhD, et al. "Short Term Improvement on a Visual-Spatial Task After Music Listening in Alzheimer's Disease: A Group Study." *Activities, Adaptation, & Aging* 26, 3 (2002) <http://www.tandfonline.com/doi/ abs/10.1300/J016v26n03_03?journalCode=waaa20#preview>.

Kaplan, Randall, et al. "Dietary Protein, Carbohydrate, and Fat Enhance Memory Performance in the Healthy Elderly." *The American Journal of Clinical Nutrition.*

Kaplan, R., E. Greenwood, G. Winocur, and Tufts University. "Breakfast Gives Memory a Boost | HealthandAge–Medical Articles and News for Health in Aging Live Well, Live Longer." *American Journal of Clinical Nutrition* 74 (2001): 687–93. *HealthandAge | Medical Articles and News for Health in*

Aging Live Well, Live Longer Health and Age, 01 Jan. 2002. <http://www
.healthandage.com/breakfast-gives-memory-a-boost>.

Kovacs, Betty MS, RD. "Diet and Nutrition Q&A by Betty Kovacs." WebMD. *Ask The Experts.* 19 Mar. 2007. MedicineNet. <http://www.medicinenet
.com/script/main/art.asp?articlekey=79871>.

Lipton, James. "Neil Simon, The Art of Theater No. 10." *The Paris Review* 125 (1992) <http://www.theparisreview.org/interviews/1994/the-art-of-theater
-no-10-neil-simon>.

Lorayne, Harry, and Jerry Lucas. *The Memory Book: The Classic Guide to Improving Your Memory at Work, at School, and at Play.* Ballantine, 1996.

Lynch, Patrick. "Semantic Memory." *Experiment Resources.* 2011. <http://www
.experiment-resources.com/semantic-memory.html>.

Mayo Clinic Staff. "Memory Loss: 7 Tips to Improve Your Memory." *Mayo Clinic.* Spring 2011 <http://www.mayoclinic.com/health/memory-loss/HA 00001>.

Medina, John. *Brain Rules: 12 Principles for Surviving and Thriving at Work, Home, and School.* Seattle: Pear Press, 2008.

"Memory Quotes." Xplore, Inc. *Memory Quotes.* BookRags Media Network. 19 March 2011. <http://www.brainyquote.com/>.

Minihan, Jennifer and Administrator. "How Food Effects Learning And Behavior | -Diet." *The Most Subtle and Profound Deficits a Child Can Have.* Isa Marrs Speech Language Pathology, PC. 13 May 2011 <http://www.where icanbeme.com/food-effects-learning-behavior/>.

National Institute On Alcohol Abuse and Alcoholism. "Alcohol's Damaging Effects On The Brain." *Alcohol Alert* 63 Oct. 2004. 74.5, (Nov. 2001): 687–93.

Nursing Assistant Central. "100 Fascinating Facts You Never Knew About the Human Brain." *Our Blog.* c. 2011. Nursing Assistant Central. 20 Mar. 2011. <http://www.nursingassistantcentral.com/>.

Olshansky, S. Jay Ph.D, et al. "A Potential Decline in Life Expectancy in the United States in the 21st Century." *The New England Journal of Medicine.* 17 Mar. 2005. <http://www.nejm.org/doi/full/10.1056/NEJMsr043743>.

Parker-Pope, Tara. "Fatty Foods Affect Memory and Exercise." *New York Times,* 13 Aug. 2009, Health sec.

Parker-Pope, Tara. "Socializing Appears to Delay Memory Problems." *Health and Wellness - Well Blog - NYTimes.com.* New York Times, 4 June 2008. <http:// well.blogs.nytimes.com/2008/06/04/socializing-appears-to-delay-memory -problems/>.

"People Who Skip Breakfast Pay a High Price." *ORB Health Sanctuary Pvt. Ltd.* Spring 2011 <http://www.indiadiets.com/Health_flash/News%20details/ skipping_breakfast.htm>.

Posit Science Corporation. "Types of Memory." Posit Science. *Types of Long-*

Term Memory. 18 Mar. 2011 <http://www.positscience.com/humanbrain/memory/types-of-memory>.

Rasolt, Daniel H. "Fatty Foods Cause Memory Loss in Diabetics: Antioxidants the Solution?" *Diabetes Foundation, Inc.* Defeat Diabetes® News, 28 June 2008. <http://www.defeatdiabetes.org/news/Default.asp?catid=&subcatid=&s=Fatty+Foods+Cause+Memory+Loss&btnSubmit=Search&all_cats=1>

Sanders, Laura. "Aerobic Exercise Boosts Memory." *Science News Magazine of the Society for Science & the Public* 2000–2011. 31 Jan. 2011 <http://www.sciencenews.org/view/generic/id/69370/title/Aerobic_exercise_boosts_memory>.

Schacter, Daniel L. *The Seven Sins of Memory: How the Mind Forgets and Remembers*. Boston: Houghton Mifflin, 2002.

Schmidt, Richard A., and Timothy D. Lee. *Motor Control and Learning a Behavioral Emphasis*. Champaign, Ill. u.a.: Human Kinetics, 2005.

United States. U.S. Department of Health and Human Services. *2008 Physical Activity Guidelines for Americans*. ODPHP Publication No. U0036, Oct. 2008.

U.S. Commerce Department figures compiled for the National Confectioners Association (NCA) and the Chocolate Manufacturers Association. (Reuters, 8/21/98).

Vintere, Parsala, et al. "Gross-Motor Skill Acquisition by Preschool Dance Students Under Self-Instruction Procedures." *Journal of Applied Behavior Analysis* 37, 305–22 (204) <http://www.ncbi.nlm.nih.gov/pmc/articles/PMC1284506/pdf/15529888.pdf>.

Willingham, Val. "The Power of Music: It's a Real Heart Opener." *Featured Articles from CNN*. CNN Health, 11 May 2009. <http://articles.cnn.com/2009-05-11/health/music.heart_1_music-therapy-laughter-study-blood-vessels?_s=PM:HEALTH>.

WWAY. "Staying Mentally Active Can Help with Memory Issues down the Road." *Wilmington NC News, Weather and Sports | WWAY NewsChannel 3 | Wwaytv3.com*. WWAY, NewsChannel 3, ABC Television Affiliate in Wilmington, North Carolina, 18 Feb. 2009. <http://www.wwaytv3.com/staying_mentally_active_can_help_memory_issues_down_road/02/2009>.